How Scotland votes

Political Analyses

Series editors: Bill Jones, Michael Clarke and Michael Moran

Roland Axtmann
Liberal democracy into the twenty-first century: globalization, integration and the nation-state

John Burton
Violence explained: the sources of conflict, violence and crime and their provention

Stuart Croft
Strategies of arms control: a history and typology

E. Franklin Dukes
Resolving public conflict: transforming community and governance

Brendan Evans and Andrew Taylor
From Salisbury to Major: continuity and change in Conservative politics

Michael Foley and John E. Owens
Congress and the Presidency: institutional politics in a separated system

How Scotland votes

votes

Scottish parties and elections

Lynn Bennie, Jack Brand and James Mitchell

Manchester University Press

Manchester and New York

distributed exclusively in the USA by St. Martin's Press

Published by Manchester University Press
Oxford Road, Manchester M13 9NR, UK
and Room 400, 175 Fifth Avenue, New York, NY 10010, USA

Distributed exclusively in the USA
by St. Martin's Press, Inc., 175 Fifth Avenue, New York,
NY 10010, USA

British Library Cataloguing-in-Publication Data
A catalogue record for this book is available from the British Library

Library of Congress Cataloging-in-Publication Data
Bennie, Lynn G.
    How Scotland votes / Lynn Bennie, Jack Brand and James Mitchell.
      p.   cm. — (Political analyses)
    ISBN 0-7190-4510-X. — ISBN 0-7190-4511-8 (pbk.)
      1. Elections–Scotland–History–20th century.   2. Scotland–
Politics and government–20th century.   3. Political parties–
Scotland–history–20th century.   I. Brand, Jack, 1934–   .
II. Mitchell, James, 1960–   . III. Title.   IV. Series.
JN1341.B46   1997
324.9411'085—dc21   96-52828
                                                                CIP

ISBN   0 7190 4510 X   *hardback*
       0 7190 4511 8   *paperback*

First published 1997

01 00 99 98 97   10 9 8 7 6 5 4 3 2 1

Printed by Redwood Books, Trowbridge

Contents

Tables

Series editors' foreword

The Politics Today series has been running successfully since the late 1970s, aimed mainly at an undergraduate audience. After over a decade in which a dozen or more titles have been produced, some of which have run to multiple copies, MUP thought it time to launch a new politics series, aimed at a different audience and a different need.

The Political Analyses series is prompted by the relative dearth of research-based political science series which persists despite the fecund source of publication ideas provided by current political developments.

In the UK we observe, for example: the rapid evolution of Labour politics as the party seeks to find a reliable electoral base; the continuing development of the post-Thatcher Conservative Party; the growth of pressure group activity and lobbying in modern British politics; and the irresistible moves towards constitutional reform of an arguably outdated state.

Abroad, there are even more themes upon which to draw, for example: the ending of the Thatcher–Reagan axis; the parallel collapse of communism in Europe and Russia; and the gradual retreat of socialism from the former heartlands in Western Europe.

This series will seek to explore some of these new ideas to a depth beyond the scope of the Politics Today series – whilst maintaining a similar direct and accessible style – and to serve an audience of academics, practitioners and the well-informed reader as well as undergraduates. The series has three editors: Bill Jones and Michael Moran, who will concentrate on domestic topics, and Michael Clarke, who will attend to international issues.

Preface

The hope of most Scots that a Scottish parliament would be established was shattered by the result of the 1992 general election. This was not the first election in which the constitutional status of Scotland was important, and doubtless will not be the last, but it was one in which the issue came near to the top of the political agenda, at least as set by the political parties. This book attempts to place this and other issues in context. Home rule is not the only issue in Scottish elections. Constitutional politics is not the only means by which Scottish politics differ from politics in England. Class, religion, economic perceptions and the image of the parties are all important: both in understanding Scotland and in understanding what makes it different. Each of these is considered in this book. Before doing this we place these in context. Scottish political behaviour, social and economic trends in Scotland and Scotland's political institutions are discussed before we consider the political behaviour of the nation.

We are grateful to the Economic and Social Research Council (ESRC) for awarding us a grant to conduct the 1992 Scottish Election Study (No. R000235290). Election studies have been conducted in Britain since 1964 (Denver 1994: 7). These are surveys conducted at election times which examine the characteristics, attitudes and behaviour patterns of the general public. Separate Scottish Election Studies were conducted in 1974, 1979 and 1992. The 1992 Scottish survey was based on a random sample of 957 voters stratified by region and drawn from fifty-nine Scottish constituencies. The fieldwork was carried out between 13 April and the beginning of September 1992 by Social and Community Planning Research. The data used in the book are largely drawn from this study plus earlier Scottish election studies, in 1974 and 1979, as well as British Election Studies. We also include election results from local and parliamentary elections in Scotland.

Scottish home rule will almost certainly feature prominently in the next election campaign. This book attempts to make sense of this and what makes Scotland politically different.

Lynn Bennie, Jack Brand and James Mitchell
November 1996

Abbreviations

AES	alternative economic strategy (of the Labour Party)
BES	British Election Study
CLPD	Campaign for Labour Party Democracy
COSLA	Convention of Scottish Local Authorities
CSA	Campaign for a Scottish Assembly
EC	European Community
EU	European Union
ILP	Independent Labour Party
LCC	Labour Coordinating Committee
NATO	North Atlantic Treaty Organisation
NPS	National Party of Scotland
NUM	National Union of Mineworkers
PLP	Parliamentary Labour Party
SDA	Scottish Development Agency
SDP	Social Democratic Party
SES	Scottish Election Study
SHRA	Scottish Home Rule Association
SLA	Scottish Labour Action
SLGIU	Scottish Local Government Information Unit
SLP	Scottish Labour Party
SNL	Scottish National League
SNM	Scottish National Movement
SNP	Scottish National Party
STUC	Scottish Trades Union Congress
SWC	Scottish Women's Caucus

1

Scotland since 1945

This chapter offers an overview of Scottish politics since 1945. The subheadings within it offer a framework which will be familiar to students of politics of almost any liberal democracy. Many of the themes and issues discussed in this book are introduced here. This will allow us to consider the extent to which Scotland is different. We have deliberately not set out to suggest that there is a British norm and to explore how Scotland diverges from it. There is no British norm, just as there is no European or liberal democratic norm. There are, however, social and political divisions commonly found in liberal democracies which are considered here.

The context in which politics operates is important and in this chapter we consider a number of themes which have been important in the development of Scotland since the war. This is by no means comprehensive but by identifying some of the most significant we have outlined the backdrop against which political parties have operated and voters have gone to the polls.

Like other parts of Europe, Scotland has changed dramatically over the last fifty years. Population movements, changes in the socio-economic structure, the process of secularisation and the changing face of industry and employment have all had an impact. Also significant has been the growing importance of external factors. International trade, inward investment and European integration have become increasingly important. Communications and the media have played a part not only in allowing Scots to have a better understanding of what happens elsewhere but also in how they see themselves. Yet, much remains the same.

Comparing the findings of an academic study of the issues involved in the 1950 general election campaign in Glasgow (Chrimes 1950) with present concerns shows the extent of continuity and degree of change in the issues of the day, at least as suggested by the political parties. It is a long time since any British government could proudly boast that it had 'ensured full employment and fair shares of the necessities of life', as

Labour's 1950 manifesto claimed. Nationalisation proved an issue in most post-war elections until fairly recently though sterling crises continue to persist and, even if not directly an issue, their consequences most certainly remain important. Planning was the great hope offered by Labour fifty years ago. The Conservatives, in opposition, were on the attack and it is significant that the term 'socialism' was more often found in Conservative literature than in material issued by the Labour Party. The level of taxation and housing, raised by Labour and the Conservatives in 1950, have remained of great importance. The Liberals' insistence on the need for proportional representation and Scottish home rule continues to dominate the agenda of its successor party though free trade has been replaced by enthusiasm for European integration. National service ended in 1960, having been an issue up to that point, thus bringing debate on it to a close, apart from the odd call for its reintroduction. The issue of equality for women remains on the agenda, though in important respects the precise demands have changed.

Before the election in 1950, a massive petition demanding a Scottish parliament had been launched. The Liberals gave it their full backing. Labour and the Conservatives were opposed. The Tories argued that Labour was centralist. A senior Tory is quoted arguing that 'Socialism means London. The centralised State must have a centre' (Chrimes 1950: 79). The poet Hugh MacDiarmid contested a Glasgow seat in the election as an independent Nationalist candidate, only to be disowned by the Scottish National Party and, more emphatically, by the organisers of the home rule petition, who sought to remain neutral, which, according to MacDiarmid, meant neutered. The team observing the election in 1950 made an interesting comment on this issue:

> Questions about Home Rule were fairly frequent at meetings everywhere, and discussion lively, but on the whole it seems that few electors put their Scottish nationalism above the chief social and economic issues of the main parties. Some Labour electors, when Home Rule was mentioned, expressed anxiety lest a Scottish Parliament should not have a Labour majority. (Chrimes 1950: 81)

Party systems and voter alignments

Looking back and comparing Scottish political behaviour over time has much value. There are problems in doing this, not least the lack of data. But change in political behaviour often comes slowly, almost imperceptibly. Comparing political behaviour over time allows us to see things which a focus on the present might miss. For this reason we have set out, so far as is possible, to compare our findings of Scotland today with Scotland in the recent past. But it is important to avoid being parochial. In most respects, Scotland is similar to other parts of Britain and, perhaps more significantly, other parts of western Europe. In order to understand Scottish political behaviour, Scotland should be placed in a wider context. Comparing Scotland with England can be useful but there is often a tendency to assume that the larger nation is the norm, that anything which makes Scotland different is an aberration. It is therefore important to work within a framework which makes no such assumptions and allows us to identify those features which are common but also unique.

The classic work of Lipset and Rokkan (1967) on party systems and voter alignments offers a framework within which a study of electoral behaviour can begin. This was a comparative European study which took account of change over time, and it identified four 'critical lines of cleavage':

> Two of these cleavages are direct products of what we might call the National Revolution: the conflict between the central nation-building culture and the increasing resistance of the ethnically, linguistically, or religiously distinct subject populations in the provinces and peripheries; the conflict between the centralizing, standardizing, and mobilizing Nation-State and the historically established privileges of the Church. Two of them are products of the Industrial Revolution: the conflict between the landed interests and the rising class of industrial entrepreneurs; the conflict between owners and employers on the one side and tenants, labourers, and workers on the other. (Lipset and Rokkan 1967: 14)

We should, therefore, look to see evidence of these political cleavages. The centre–periphery cleavage might be expected to be found in Scotland where an historic nation, with distinct institutions and a sense of itself, exists. We should also note that a centre–periphery cleavage might be found within Scotland. Interests might be found in Scotland's (post-)industrial central belt which differ from those of the more remote, rural parts of the country. It has been the case that third parties (any of the smaller parties in a traditionally two-party system) have found it easier to advance, retain support or rekindle old support in the Highlands, islands and border regions of Scotland. It should also be noted that in 1992 the Conservatives did better in the north-east of Scotland. This may well have reflected the more buoyant nature of the local economy at the time.

Religion too might be expected to have played a part in political attitudes, perhaps in a different manner from that found elsewhere but evident nonetheless. The rise of urban Scotland and the interests this spawned may well have given rise to an urban–rural conflict, though that may have been more pertinent in an earlier age. We should expect to find evidence of the class cleavage if only because Lipset and Rokkan found this to have been the most significant in recent times and also because

Scotland was at the forefront of the industrial revolution in Europe, and that revolution gave rise to class politics.

Lipset and Rokkan maintained that a 'hierarchy of cleavage bases' exists which will not only vary from one country to the next but also will vary within any country over time. The relationship between the different cleavages is important. Whether one cleavage cuts or reinforces another cleavage may change over time. It is conceivable that the rise of class politics would replace centre–periphery divisions. Alternatively, these two may reinforce one another.

Since their work was published, others have, or claim to have, discovered new cleavages. Ronald Inglehart argued that in societies in which basic material needs have been met there has been a shift towards post-material values. This is evident among different generations. Post-materialists can be expected to be found among those whose early political experiences have been formed at a time of relative growth and will place less emphasis on economic growth and more emphasis on non-economic quality-of-life concerns including support for the environment or European integration (Inglehart 1977, 1990). Russell Dalton distinguished between old and new politics. Old politics are based on 'traditional political alignments', primarily class. New political cleavages involve a new set of political concerns including protecting the environment, minority rights, greater democratisation and other 'new left' issues (Dalton 1988, 1996). These concerns have emerged in Europe in the form of new social movements (Müller-Rommel 1989; Dalton and Kuechler 1990). Dalton describes the formation of a new cleavage around a coalition of 'student protesters and the women's movement' (Dalton 1988: 138). However, unlike other west European states, new-left groups have had only a limited impact in Britain.

Events, agendas and trends

The cleavage structures discussed above operate at a level of abstraction and it is important to make them concrete. Events are one way of illustrating the importance of cleavages. Identifying some of the key events and watersheds which affected Scottish political behaviour is tricky. Some of the most significant changes have arisen gradually, almost imperceptibly, and the list of watersheds and trends affecting Scottish political behaviour is extensive.

What is significant in looking back over the last fifty years is just how rarely the key temporal benchmarks have been associated with elections. In an essay published in 1988, David Butler, doyen of British election scholars, made this point:

> What do elections decide? Do they decide anything? It may sound cynical, after a lifetime largely devoted to the study of elections, to argue that

elections seldom set the fate of the nation. But there are some worrying facts. Think of the major events of the last forty years: the convertibility crisis of 1947; the devaluation of 1949; the Korean war of 1950; the Suez crisis of 1956; the first try for Europe in 1962; the second try in 1967; the devaluation of 1967; the third try in 1972; the IMF crisis in 1976; even the Falklands war of 1982. Not one of these phenomena was actually associated with an election, or a change of government. In almost all cases there must be a strong suspicion that if the other party had been in power at the time, events could have taken much the same course. (Butler 1988: 78)

It is difficult to avoid agreeing with Butler though at least two elections can be seen as watersheds: 1945 and 1979. Arguably it was not only the elections themselves which made them watersheds but their context, one coming towards the end of the war and the other at a time of economic disruption. Perhaps more significant have been trends. It is possible to identify a number of issues and trends which have shaped modern Scotland and had an impact on political attitudes. These are discussed below.

The welfare state

The development of the welfare state has had profound implications. The social structure of Scotland has been affected and the life opportunities of many Scots have increased. Also, a new class of people associated with the management and servicing of the welfare state has grown up. This has been reflected in the trade unions as well as the wider labour force. White-collar employment linked to public-sector employment – in health, housing and education – has grown since 1945. So, on the one hand we may have witnessed a lessening of the class divide in the sense that the gulf between rich and poor has declined since 1945, not withstanding any reversals in the process since the mid-1970s, but there has been a corresponding growth in the number of people whose livelihood is tied to the welfare state.

The development of the welfare state has had wide repercussions. The creation of a better-educated electorate might be expected to lead to a weakening of traditional ties – increasing secularisation, a weakening of class identification and a dealignment in political identification with the two dominant parties. However, the growth of huge public-sector housing schemes is sometimes presented as the creation of corrals of voting fodder for Labour.

Returning to the Lipset and Rokkan schema, the welfare state might be seen as affecting the class cleavage in politics. But it was more complex than that. The welfare state offered a new reason for feeling a sense of belonging; it provided a new set of British institutions. Aneurin Bevan personified this well: the founder of the National Health Service, a Welsh-man by birth, was quite contemptuous of Welsh nationalism. Bevan, and indeed the welfare state, was fairly centralist and avowedly British. From the left, here was something British worth preserving and protecting. The British welfare state probably more than the Empire helped cement the union – and certainly for working-class Scots it offered more than the Empire ever had.

Significantly, the issue of welfare, which had proved part of the cement for most of the post-war period, came to undermine Britain in the 1980s. Perceptions that the welfare state was under threat seemed to have played their part in making the case for greater autonomy. This came after 1979 – the notion that the Scotland Act 1978 would act as a bulwark against attacks on welfare were heard only after the referendum. For an increasing number of Scots, support for a Scottish parliament has rested on supporting the same state: the welfare state.

Urban and regional planning

The post-war period was a period of planning. Legislation passed by Attlee's Labour government empowered the Scottish Office to engage in strategic planning as never before. Local authorities played their part too. New towns and peripheral schemes were developed. One consequence was the loss of population from the cities, but Scottish cities retained their central place in Scottish politics. In the United States, the cities lost importance and America became, politically, a suburban country: the suburbs and their interests came to dominate the politics of the country as a whole. In England, too, there is evidence of this. But despite the loss of population from the cities, the cities still count for much in Scottish politics.

The new towns and peripheral schemes in the 1960s proved fertile ground for the Nationalists. This may have been a factor in the Labour government's decision to abandon the plan to develop Stonehouse New Town in the mid-1970s, but it was secondary. By then the dangers of abandoning the cities, in particular Glasgow, were becoming apparent. The 'rediscovery of poverty' in the 1960s and the 1971 census had shown the extent of 'multiple deprivation' in urban areas. The Glasgow East Area Renewal Scheme replaced Stonehouse and, while it failed to reverse economic decline, it marked a new era in which the city was to come to the fore again in the concerns of the Scottish Office. Indeed, some would argue that rural and small-town Scotland lost out in the process. The cities, and Glasgow in particular, did relatively well in terms of public funding from the mid-1970s.

It would be wrong to suggest that there was a strong urban–rural split in Scottish politics, especially if by that was meant any reference to the cleavage identified by Lipset and Rokkan. On the other hand, a feature of post-war politics which suggested that such a division did exist is to be found in party political support in different parts of Scotland. Conservative decline involved a departure from Glasgow, which allowed Labour to dominate the city. Conservatives rarely performed well in Dundee. In Aberdeen they usually managed to hold one of the city's two seats (Labour won both in 1966 and in 1983). In Edinburgh the Conservatives maintained their hold from 1950, winning four of the capital's seven seats (then six from 1983) before the Conservative collapse in 1987, when they were reduced to two, which they held in 1992.

The politics of farming areas have been fairly self-contained but the absence of a perception of a different set of interests between urban and rural areas prevented such a divide taking on political salience after 1945. This does not mean that support for the parties should be the same throughout Scotland. The Liberal Democrats and Scottish National Party (SNP) have managed to break through in parts of rural Scotland but not in urban areas; however, this does not necessarily represent a sharp urban–rural cleavage.

Religion and politics

In the sense that Lipset and Rokkan identified, religion has played a less significant part in Scottish politics than elsewhere. In the twentieth century religion has been evident but it has been linked to questions of immigration. Anti-Catholic sentiment was based on opposition to Irish immigration. However vehement the theological views of Scots Presbyterian ministers and Kirk general-assembly debates appear to have been, for the public at large anti-Catholicism involved opposition to 'foreigners'. The integration without assimilation of Irish Catholics into Scottish society was the result of a number of factors. The relative prosperity of Scotland meant that jobs were less scarce than in the pre-war period, which reduced social tensions. The 1918 Education Act, one of the most progressive and enlightened measures to be passed by the Scottish Office, allowed for integration and provided opportunities for social and economic advancement for the Catholic community. The Labour Party, which represented the interests of this substantial section of the Catholic community in Scotland, helped the integration process. Another view is that the decline of shipbuilding and other heavy industries destroyed social milieus in which sectarianism had been maintained through employment practices. Additionally, many communities in Glasgow which had a sectarian base were uprooted as new towns and peripheral schemes were built to rehouse overcrowded inner cities.

Scottish politics for most of the post-war period were particularly dichotomised among the working class, with Catholics tending overwhelmingly to vote Labour and a substantial proportion of Protestants voting Conservative/Unionist, though by no means as many as is sometimes suggested. But compared with elsewhere in Europe, this was not so unusual. What was strikingly unusual was that the Catholic community voted for the party of the left, but that reflected the social and economic status of what had been a fairly recent immigrant community.

The change which has occurred has been in the Conservative vote. The Conservative Party lost its working-class Protestant vote without any compensating gain among middle-class Catholics. Labour meanwhile held on to its Catholic support and made gains among working-class Protestants. The fact that this dichotomy was breaking down by the 1960s was fortunate for the SNP, making it easier for this 'new party' to pick up support, especially where it was dealigning from its traditional support. It also meant that the SNP had the greatest difficulty in attracting support where the traditional attachment of Catholics to the Labour Party still remained strong. It is only in very recent elections that evidence has emerged of some loosening in this attachment.

Since the war, religious identification and the vote has been significant but for one section of the community it has weakened. The Protestant working class are no longer, if they ever really were, a cohesive political force. We can no longer be so confident in predicting voting intentions by religion.

From central economic management to economic decline

Alec Cairncross has written that economic planning was one of the 'first ideas to surface at the end of the war' (Cairncross 1992: 2). Tied to such notions as 'modernisation', planning and central economic management kept being reinvented throughout the post-war period. Scots looked increasingly to the state for their homes, schooling and also their jobs. High expectations of the state were simply not realised. Arguably this has played its part in the decline in confidence in institutions closely associated with the state, including the established parties.

Alongside the revaluations of sterling signalling problems in the British economy from 1949 to 1967 to the decision to withdraw from the Exchange Rate Mechanism in 1992, there have been a number of blows which have affected an export-based economy such as Scotland's. In 1978 Sir Douglas Wass, then Permanent Secretary at the Treasury, pointed out that the trend towards international economic integration was the 'single most important structural change in the world economy in the second half of the twentieth century' (Cairncross 1992: 295). As Cairncross has pointed out, the 'fundamental change' affecting Britain in this period was 'a loss of economic power: commercial power, bargaining power, financial power. Britain had become a much smaller fragment of the world economy with much less influence on the behaviour of that economy' (Cairncross 1992: 286).

Perhaps the key event affecting the Scottish economy over the period was caused by war in the Middle East. The Yom Kippur War of 1973/4 caused a quadrupling of the price of oil overnight with devastating consequences for Western economies and ultimately for politics too. In Britain, it made coal an even more valuable commodity and allowed the miners to take on the Heath government successfully. The year 1974 saw two elections and despite the obvious importance of class as an underlying issue, as played out through the industrial relations question, particularly in February, the nationalist dimension also came to the fore with the SNP making its breakthrough. Contrary to what might have been expected, the election saw two major cleavages – class and nationality – forcing their way forward simultaneously on to the political agenda, both provoked or encouraged by the same external events. Energy and oil had arrived as political issues even though the oil itself was not to appear in quantity until after 1979.

Oil did not cause the rise of nationalism so much as give the case for self-government greater credibility. The earlier energy crisis may have been more important in helping to undermine the notion of British 'greatness'. Britain staggered from crisis to crisis in the late 1970s, sterling 'nearly died' as headlines later expressed it, and Britain was the sick man of Europe. The conditions for disaffection with Britain were great.

But the SNP was not the beneficiary. Even if structural conditions appeared to be conducive to the rise of the SNP, the party was unable to take, or incapable of taking, advantage. The lack of an overall majority for the Labour government within a short period of time placed the new and inexperienced SNP MPs in the invidious position of working in Westminster under the intense gaze of the media and public. Their equally inexperienced and even less adroit colleagues in local government conveyed a less than favourable impression. The luxury of basking in opposition was not really available to the Nationalists, who became almost as tied up in the politics of crisis management and British economic decline, at least in public perceptions, as the Labour Party. So, the opportunity offered by British economic decline was not taken advantage of by the Nationalists. It was the Conservatives under their radical new leader Margaret Thatcher who took full advantage.

The 1979 election was to be a watershed election not because Margaret Thatcher won but because of the opportunities afforded by North Sea oil. If ever there were elections which, with hindsight, no party would have wanted to win given the difficulties which then lay ahead it would have been those in 1974. The 1979 election was quite different. The trickle of oil coming ashore at St Fergus became a gushing torrent. An opportunity now existed. But Margaret Thatcher had no intention of carrying on where Labour left off. She had her own agenda and one set, again, in the context of the UK's economic decline. Reading her memoirs (Thatcher 1993) and observing the *Thatcherfest* in the media around the same time, the most striking aspect seems to have been her desire to 'reverse decline'.

Employment, labour relations and post-materialism

Unemployment became an issue in Scotland before it emerged centre stage south of the border. In May 1959, unemployment rose to 116,000, with the ending of national service and deflation. Regional policy was pursued. In 1963 Gavin McCrone identified four periods in British regional policy: active, 1945–51; passive, 1951–8; transition, 1959–62; and sustained, 1963 onwards. Looking back in 1996, we can identify a further three periods since 1963: sustained, 1963 to mid-1970s; demise, mid-1970s to 1979; and gradual abandonment, since 1979.

Regional policy had little success in protecting Scotland from the series of economic crises which have affected the British and Scottish economies since the war. Certainly new jobs were brought to Scotland through regional policy and inward investment helped, but the trend remained one of increasing unemployment, especially as compared with Britain as a whole for most of the post-war period. Only with the advent of economic crises in the 1980s did Scotland's relative position improve. England declined at a faster rate than Scotland during the UK's later economic decline.

What is notable is that the areas affected by unemployment were the highly unionised heavy industries. The popular perception of Scotland as an economy based on heavy industries with a political culture infused with militant trade unionism was becoming increasingly unrealistic. With the passing of the heavy industries, the dominance in trade union and Labour politics of related issues declined, to be replaced by white-collar unionism, with the dominance in employment terms of the financial services and banking, but, curiously, the myth of Scotland as a place where heavy industries still dominate seems to prevail in certain quarters. The power of myth seems difficult to get away from in Scotland. Today, the Crofters' Union has more members than the National Union of Mineworkers (NUM) yet the political culture suggests otherwise.

It is tempting to portray the period before 1979 as one of consensus, but in industrial relations it is difficult to do this. Labour relations troubled successive governments from the 1960s. From Barbara Castle's white paper *In Place of Strife* in 1969 and Ted Heath's Industrial Relations Act 1971, labour relations caused governments problems. Many of these problems focused on Scotland. Clydeside's reputation for radicalism was reinforced with the Upper Clyde Shipbuilders dispute when the workforce briefly took over the shipyard. The myth of 'Red Clydeside' seemed to require some new event each generation to rekindle the flame.

Inglehart has suggested that support for environmentalism and European integration have resulted in a post-materialist age. This 'new politics' cleavage, however, appears to have had little impact in Scotland. The Scottish Green Party had a brief period of electoral success at the end of the 1980s[1] but compared with green parties in other west European countries (Richardson and Rootes 1995) it has failed to make a major impression. This probably has as much to do with an unfavourable electoral system and a competitive party system as lack of support for the Greens. The environmental movement as a whole has had some success in pushing issues nearer to the top of the political agenda.

It might be tempting to suggest that Scottish nationalism is an example of post-materialism; that would be quite wrong. The SNP's nationalism is materialist. Its propaganda has focused on materialist concerns; their message is 'It's Scotland's oil' not 'Save our heritage'.

There have been changes. Since the war the central concern has been materialist but those pursuing materialism through work have increasingly included women. There is more part-time employment, and far fewer Scots are employed in large plants where social contacts are believed to play a significant part in developing political attitudes.

From consensus to Thatcherism

The arrival of Margaret Thatcher is often seen as the end of consensus politics in Britain. We have to be careful here and not look back to a 'golden age that never was'. Nonetheless, there is ample evidence that some degree of consensus did exist before the mid-1970s. As far as Scotland is concerned there is one aspect of this which is worth mentioning which rarely, if ever, is mentioned in the literature on consensus. It is a consensus which predates 1945, though after then there were claims by parties when in opposition that it had been abandoned by their opposite number in government.

This consensus concerned the status of Scotland within the union. While the rhetoric and practice of parliamentary sovereignty ruled out the prospect of self-government, each party accepted that Scotland should be treated as a distinct nation and not merely a region of Britain. This was best expressed in the work of Rokkan and Urwin when they distinguished between a unitary state and a union state. The former suggests uniformity around a strong centralised system of government. The latter was defined as follows:

> not the result of straightforward dynastic conquest. Incorporation of at least parts of its territory has been achieved through personal dynastic union, for example by treaty, marriage or inheritance. Integration is less than perfect. While administrative standardisation prevails over most of the territory, the consequences of personal union entail the survival in some areas of pre-union rights and institutional infrastructures which preserve some degree of regional autonomy and serve as agencies of indigenous elite recruitment. (Rokkan and Urwin 1982: 11)

---

1   In the 1989 elections to the European parliament the Scottish Greens received 7.2 per cent of the votes cast. The Greens in the UK overall achieved 14.9 per cent.

Over time, this has been manifested in different ways but ultimately some degree of Scottish distinctiveness has been permitted. Margaret Thatcher saw Scotland as part of a unitary state rather than a union state. She neither understood nor attempted to understand the consensual view that Scotland has a distinct place in the union. But there was even more to it than that. In the context of her critique of the UK's economic decline, Scotland had a special part.

Margaret Thatcher had taken on board at least part of a critique of British government which the American political historian Sam Beer called 'pluralistic stagnation' (Beer 1982: 24–6). Beer, in his *Modern British Politics*, first published in 1965, had been a great defender of the British political system but was having doubts by the early 1980s. In *Britain Against Itself*, published in 1982, Beer was more pessimistic and maintained that stagnation was resulting from the large number of interests making demands on the political system. Margaret Thatcher accepted a particular form of this critique; it was not so much the number but the nature and aggressiveness of some groups which were causing problems. Trade unions were particularly focused on but so too, in a sense, was Scotland.

The special status accorded to Scotland became unacceptable to Margaret Thatcher. In her early years she permitted 'wets' to dominate her cabinet including the wettest of all – George Younger. That was not to last and towards the end of his time as Scottish Secretary, longer than any other in the history of the office, evidence that Thatcher saw Scotland as part of a unitary state became increasingly evident. In public-expenditure discussions, in debates on the future of key industries and in pushing through social legislation, there seemed every sign that the Conservatives saw the notion of the union state as at best a luxury. In the rhetoric of Thatcherism, Scottish interests assumed the status of one of those pressure groups which had been overburdening the British state. Her comments on the Scottish Office in her memoirs are significant:

> The pride of the Scottish Office – whose very structure added a layer of bureaucracy, standing in the way of the reforms which were paying such dividends in England – was that public expenditure per head in Scotland was far higher than in England. (Thatcher 1993: 627)

From Empire to Europe

The decline of Empire has been a gradual process. It has had a number of repercussions. At one level it has forced Scots to consider the nature of their Britishness. This is also now under way in England but in a more particular manner and more recently. In England some of the most interesting debates around the decline of Empire and its implications for British politics and culture have focused on the politics of race and immigration: such work considers the identities of immigrants in Britain. In Scotland the debate has focused on the place of Scotland within Britain.

The shock to Britain's sense of its position in the world was most marked following the Suez crisis in 1956. The repercussions of this single event were considerable. The immediate need had been to rebuild relations with the United States (Young 1993: 51–2) and a distancing from France – making even less likely Britain's early involvement in the emerging European Economic Community. However, in time the 'three circles' concept (Britain operated within three circles: America and the Atlantic; the Commonwealth; and Europe – in that order) was undermined. Perhaps at the level of popular opinion, the notion of British greatness was suspect and it would be understandable if that was the case in Scotland. If so, the party or parties most closely associated with that version of Britishness would expect to face difficulties. At elite level, however, the notion of British greatness remained central (Holland 1991).

Membership of the European Union (EU) can probably be seen in these terms too. The attempt to salvage Britain's position in the world and to find a market for its goods motivated membership. Scots were, of course, highly critical of the European Community (EC) before and after joining, though a majority did vote to stay in at the 1975 referendum. Membership of the EU has offered a new focus for Scots. To date, however, Scotland's relations with the EU have replicated Scotland's relations with Whitehall: it is seen as a source of funds. The experience of Scottish politicians as 'pork-barrel' politicians in British terms has proved useful in dealings with Europe.

The role of women

In many respects, Scotland is intensely conservative. The proportion of women elected to public office is very low. This does not mean that women have played a limited role in Scottish politics. Much political activity is hidden from view or, at least, not conducted in the glare of publicity. Much of this work is done by women. Women have played a significant part in grass-roots campaigns in tenants' associations, community councils, in campaigning against the poll tax, against hospital and school closures. Between 1945 and 1992, the peak of women's representation in parliament from Scotland was five, in 1959 and 1964. The election which brought Margaret Thatcher to power as Britain's first woman Prime Minister saw the return of only one woman MP from a Scottish constituency. Five were returned in 1992 but the election of Helen Liddell and Roseanna Cunningham in by-elections pushed the total to its wartime high of seven (out of seventy-two).

There has long been a higher proportion of women councillors in Scotland, partly reflecting the active involvement of women in grass-roots politics. Over a fifth of councillors elected to the new unitary authorities in 1995 were women.

For a brief period, during John Smith's leadership, Labour was committed to positive action to tackle this imbalance but otherwise the political parties have been reluctant to confront the gross under-representation of Scottish women. The political parties have yet to go much beyond acknowledging that a problem exists.

A study by Brown (referred to in Brown *et al.*, 1996: 170–3) suggested there are a number of impediments in the way of women standing for parliament: the location of parliament in London, its antisocial hours, the first-past-the-post electoral system were all identified. Party rules and organisation, including timing of meetings, were seen as impediments. Women's role in the family was a key impediment identified but lack of resources was seen as less important than other studies had found. A 'predominantly male culture' in Scotland was cited as an inhibiting factor. The 'macho, adversarial style and ethos of politics' was seen as significant (Brown *et al.* 1996: 173).

Much hope has been placed on the possibility that a Scottish parliament would bring more women into politics. Debates within the Labour and Liberal Democratic parties, separately and jointly in the Constitutional Convention, concluded in favour of the principle of fifty–fifty representation of men and women but no agreement could be reached as to how this would be achieved. For any Scottish parliament to realise the hopes of those seeking increased women's participation in politics, it would need to make a breakthrough in women's representation from the start. Even if a more consensual style were to be adopted, and its location proved advantageous, these would not necessarily be enough to overcome the deeply ingrained male culture of Scottish politics.

Mediating influences

One reason for the failure of 'new politics' in Britain may be that politics does not take place in a vacuum. Similar forces may help shape political behaviour across Europe, but politics is mediated through institutions such as the electoral system, political parties, press and television. According to the diffusionist school of thought, many of these mediating influences would be expected to lead to a greater degree of uniformity and the decline of centre–periphery conflicts. As news filters through to the public through the same television channels and newspapers selling throughout the state, the same information, same views and same interpretation of what is important would reduce regional diversity. Political parties operating on a British basis would be expected to serve a similar function. But this has not happened. Nonetheless, mediating influences have had a considerable impact on Scottish political behaviour. These include the electoral system, the press, television and radio, and, of course, the political parties.

The electoral system

The first-past-the-post electoral system is notoriously disproportional, as losers under the system constantly point out. It has proved a major impediment in the way of new and third parties. It is worth noting, however, that the system was not always disproportional. Indeed, at the high point of two-party politics, in the 1950s, it was highly proportional. This highlights an important, though often overlooked, fact: the *principle* of proportionality should not be confused with *electoral systems*. Apart from the national list system, the proportionality of an electoral system may differ over time. So, we find that the degree of (dis)proportionality has changed over the post-war period in Scotland. Calculations of the degree of proportionality exist.[2]

Over the post-war period, the high point of proportionality was in 1955, at the height of the two-party system, and its low point was in 1992 (Figure 1.1). The Labour Party has benefited most. At each election its percentage share of Scottish seats has exceeded its percentage share of the vote. But the Conservatives have not been so fortunate. The Conservative share of Scottish seats has fallen below their share of the vote on all but four occasions since 1945 – in 1950, 1951, 1955 and 1983. In ten of the fourteen elections, the Conservatives have lost out under the first-past-the-post electoral system in Scotland. In 1992, the Conservatives had more reason

---

2   The one we have used is that of Loosemore and Hanby (1971). A figure can be arrived at for each election. Deviation from proportionality in Scotland in the 1992 election was 29.1, calculated using the following formula:

$$D = \frac{1}{2} \Sigma \, |si - vi|$$

where D stands for deviation from proportionality; Σ stands for summation over all parties involved; si stands for seats; and vi stands for votes. Below is how it works:

Party	% of seats	% of votes	Difference (seats–votes)
Conservative	15.3	25.7	-10.4
Labour	68.1	39.0	+29.1
Liberal Democrat	12.5	13.1	-0.6
SNP	4.2	21.5	-17.3
Others	0.0	0.0	-0.8

Sum of moduli = 58.2
Deviation from proportionality = 29.1

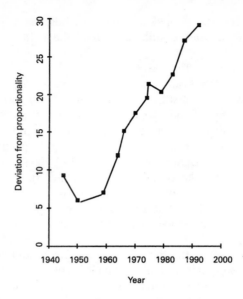

Figure 1.1. Deviation from proportionality in the results of general elections in Scotland.

to curse the system than the Liberal Democrats, though they greatly benefited from it in Britain as a whole, while the SNP has consistently had most to complain about.

Electoral systems are important not only in translating public support into political representation. They can have other mediating effects. An electoral system can conspire to make a party appear weaker than its support suggests and thus can damage its credibility. Gaining credibility is an important first step in maximising popularity. It must also be remembered that political parties, especially new and small parties, are largely amateur organisations, heavily reliant on members being elected to public office to give them full-time politicians. MPs provide parties with full-time propagandists but since the 1970s and the introduction of 'Short money'[3] in the Commons, they also have back-up with full-time staff. For small parties this can make a big difference. The electoral system can be a conservative influence, helping to ossify a political system, preventing new political cleavages manifesting themselves by setting a high threshold for political representation. The electoral system may be less a mediating factor and

---

3   'Short money' was named after Ted Short, Labour Leader of the House of Commons, who introduced this support for political parties in March 1975.

more a militating factor. Scottish party politics has shown that under the first-past-the-post system, parties need to concentrate their vote or to win over 30 per cent of an evenly spread share of support to make a major breakthrough.

The press

The overwhelming support for the Conservatives in the British press, particularly among the tabloids, has been part of the explanation for successive Conservative victories in Britain since 1979 (Dunleavy and Husbands 1985; Harrop 1986; Miller 1991; Curtice and Semetko 1994). In some ways, the Scottish situation lends support to the proposition that, as the headline of the *Sun* (English, not Scottish, edition) put it after the 1992 election, 'It was the *Sun* wot won it'. The anti-Tory stance of the Scottish press is a frequent complaint from Conservative politicians north of the border and might help to explain the Labour Party's impressive performance.

The most significant aspect of the press in Scotland is its Scottishness. Benedict Anderson laid great stress on the role of the print media in creating 'imagined communities' in his work on nationalism (Anderson 1991). Since the war, a healthy, even stubborn, Scottish press has continued to exist. As well as Scottish national papers there is also a vibrant Scottish local press. Modern technology and communications have, if anything, assisted the continued survival of the Scottish media.

Whether the Scottish press projects an accurate picture of Scotland is doubtful. Ian Bell, who edited perhaps the most exciting but short-lived Scottish Sunday supplement, supplied by the *Observer* in the late 1980s, warned that the Scottish press 'for decades, perhaps for centuries, acted as a distorting mirror ... the Scottish media as a whole have been complicit in the denial of the Scottish identity and have as an ironic consequence, laid the seeds of their own destruction' (Bell 1993: 387). A less apocalyptic view is expressed by a former editor of the *Scotsman*, who notes the great variety in the Scottish press with over 160 titles, including local papers (Linklater 1992: 127).

A charge often made against the Scottish press is that it has fomented political nationalism. There is no doubt that proprietors and editors have in the past used the Scottish dimension in battles for increased sales, from Beaverbrook in the 1930s with the *Scottish Daily Express* and its endorsement of Scottish nationalism to Rupert Murdoch's *Sun* endorsing Scottish independence in Europe in January 1992. Commercial reasons probably outweighed political considerations on these occasions but a market was perceived to exist – it was not created by the papers. Research on the period 1966–78, when the SNP rose to some prominence, would suggest that the Scottish press followed events rather than led them (Stovall 1978).

Harvie has noted the changes in ownership of the Scottish daily press over the twentieth century (Harvie 1993: 123). There has been a marked decline both in the number of papers on sale and in the proportion owned in Scotland, from twenty papers in 1920 all under Scottish ownership to fifteen in 1992 with only four under Scottish ownership, two owned from England and nine owned by multinationals; the Scottish press has followed a pattern common elsewhere. More important than ownership is editorial control.

There have been remarkable changes in this respect since the war. All the main Scottish newspapers, apart from the *Daily Record* and *Sunday Mail*, were Tory supporting until the late 1950s. The message was overwhelmingly Scottish but equally overwhelmingly unionist. The *Scotsman* became Liberal after it was bought by Roy Thomson in 1953 and flirted with nationalism in the mid-1970s. But since 1945, the *Scotsman* has struggled both commercially and to maintain its reputation as a first-class newspaper, at least compared with its heyday in the nineteenth century. Even so, in 1963 it was voted one of the three best newspapers in Britain and among the best twenty in the world by a panel of American professors of journalism (Stovall 1978: 61–2). The *Glasgow Herald* was traditionally the business community's paper and fairly right of centre for most of the post-war period. A drift to the centre became evident in the mid-1970s and it endorsed home rule in 1975 having previously been a staunch critic. In the 1980s it abandoned any residual sympathy for Conservatism and Unionism.

The Aberdeen *Press and Journal*, most remarkable for its different editions offering highly localised news coverage, moved away from the Conservatives in the late 1960s and has since moved between support for the Liberals and the SNP, though in recent years it has been fairly antagonistic towards the Nationalists. The *Courier and Advertiser*, based in Dundee and part of the D. C. Thomson empire, has proved remarkably resilient to change. Only slightly less so than its sister paper the *Sunday Post*, the *Courier* has been Conservative and couthy. It is a paper from a different era, though modern technology is used. Its success rests on its local appeal and ability to produce a number of different editions for different parts of Scotland, demonstrating that the modern world of mass communications facilitates rather than denies the encouragement of localness. Predictions of a global media spewing out the same message throughout the world have been disproved in Scotland as elsewhere.

Most notably, the rise of the tabloids has seen the rise of the Labour-supporting press in Scotland. The *Daily Record* has come to dominate the Scottish scene though its rise only came in the 1960s. Until then it had lagged behind the *Scottish Daily Express*. Beaverbrook's plan after buying the *Express* in 1916 had been to build printing works in Manchester and

Glasgow to take advantage of what he saw as a growing market. The closure of the Glasgow plant in 1974 proved damaging for the paper. With its removal from Scotland, the *Express* also removed sympathy for the Scottish dimension, especially after becoming a tabloid in 1977 and shortly thereafter being sold to Trafalgar House.

The most notable recent development has been the rise of the *Sun*. Rupert Murdoch's *Sun* was, of course, staunchly Conservative and epitomised the vulgarity of Fleet Street (though the term has since become a misnomer). The *Sun*'s endorsement of 'independence in Europe' in January 1992 stemmed from the same motivation which had led to the launch of its Scottish edition and the opening of its Kinning Park premises; it was targeting a very clear market, one where there was an absence of competition. The most striking aspect of mass-circulation papers in Scotland over the last twenty years has been the absence of any real competition; the *Record* had it very easy for a long time. What is notable is the commercial faith the *Sun* had in abandoning a populist pro-Conservative message in Scotland and targeting a largely young, male, working-class market with a nationalist message. There is little doubt that commercial reasoning dominated the decision. The view that it was a plot to help the Conservatives, which gained currency at the time, says something about the almost paranoid response of its main competitor and lack of any meaningful competition until fairly recently.

Television and radio

The first BBC television broadcast in Scotland was in March 1952. Back then there were 41,000 television sets in Scotland; within a decade there were 1,119,000 (Harvie 1993: 140). Now 98 per cent of households in Scotland have at least one television set (Central Statistical Office 1995). Scottish Television began broadcasting in 1955. David Butler maintains that 1959 was the first 'television election' and has maintained that the advent of television has been the most important change affecting elections since 1945 (Butler 1993). Politicians now have faces and not just names or voices. The BBC in the early post-war period was stuffy and establishment. Between 1933 and 1957, under the guidance of the Reverend Melville Dinwiddie, BBC Scotland became a 'by-word for puritanical parochialism' (Harvie 1993: 128). It was not until 1967/8 that both BBC Scotland and STV began transmitting serious political programmes but the main news and current affairs output continued to come from London. This is notable at election time, when strict rules apply which make elections very British affairs.

While the broadcast media based in Scotland were accused of fuelling the rise of nationalism in the 1970s by anti-home-rulers, they have tended to follow rather than lead opinion. At the height of interest in the Scottish dimension in the late 1970s, there were great tensions within the BBC.

Alastair Hetherington's account of his period as controller of BBC Scotland is both a frank and a fascinating account of London–Scottish relations within a public institution and can be interpreted as a metaphor of Scottish public life for the era, with all its high hopes and false dawns (Hetherington 1992).

Broadcasting, like the print media, has also produced a highly localised form. Radio Scotland came into existence as a separate broadcasting station only in 1974 though, in effect, it had existed before then as an opt-out service from Radio 4 (McDowell 1992: 209). The development of independent local radio has provided Scotland with something comparable to its local press: a variety of local outlets owned by a few. West Sound, serving Ayrshire, was the last truly independent local radio station. The owners of Radio Clyde now control local radio stations covering the Clyde, Forth, Tay, the Borders, the Northeast and West Sound.

Whether we see the media in Scotland as either transmitter or shaper of Scottish political values and opinion, they are today concentrated in fewer hands than in the past but, ironically, offer a more diverse output. While there has certainly been an internationalisation of output ('Americanisation' would perhaps be more accurate), there remains a resilient and robust Scottish dimension. In terms of news and current affairs, the communications revolution has seen the Scottish dimension increased over the post-war period but that has reflected rather than been caused by the changing politics of the country.

The role of the parties

A theme which emerged in the 1980s literature in electoral studies was the need to reassess the role of political parties. In some studies parties were seen almost as passive, the recipients of votes delivered by a social system and economic forces. The work of Heath *et al.* (1985, 1991) stressed the need to consider whether parties themselves might not be important.

Party strategies do help explain much. Labour's concentration on its urban and central-belt core of support may well explain why it now does poorly in much of rural Scotland. Labour's image as an urban party with spokesmen (usually men) from the central belt making references to central-belt matters would not endear them to the Highlands and Borders. There is no doubt that this image was played upon by opponents of devolution in the late 1970s. Ultimately, however, Labour in Scotland has a highly efficient vote; concentrating its attentions has paid dividends.

The Conservative Party seems to have been incapable of maintaining its hold on its old coalition of support or finding a new coalition from the 1960s. The Party has seemed at a loss as to what to do for the last thirty years or so. It seems to be difficult to avoid the conclusion that the Conservative Party in Scotland has been its own worst enemy. The main problem for the Party is its 'dependency culture': Scottish Tories have come to depend on their English colleagues succeeding. The life has gone out of the Party and there is as yet no sign of it returning. The prospect of complete annihilation seemed to concentrate minds, but that creeping dependency has reasserted itself again.

The Liberals and Liberal Democrats have proved remarkably resilient, holding seats against the trend. But the problem for the Party in Scotland over the post-war period is that they have failed to develop a coherent and convincing collective identity. The profile of Liberal Democrat voters is a confused one and in some ways quite at odds with the Party's own policies and positions. In essence the Liberal Democrats are a party of 'local heroes'. That is the basis of their electoral success where it has been achieved.

The SNP has had a similar problem. It has had a fairly incoherent collective image. It has appeared opportunistic in its approach. But the main problem the SNP has faced, common to third parties working in first-past-the-post systems, is that it has failed to concentrate its support. The SNP's electoral strategy has been like a blunderbuss: it has fired its shot into the air and scored a few hits but has made little impact. A more precise or refined approach might have paid dividends but impatience and a belief in its own rhetoric (and this dates back to the 1960s, not just 1992) has been its own undoing.

Conclusion

In terms of the discussion of cleavages, the significance of religion has declined (it was never quite the cleavage in Scotland as Lipset and Rokkan meant anyway). The urban–rural divide has had some relevance but not much. Much of Scotland is semi-urban/semi-rural; it is small town. That has inevitably prevented the rise of such a cleavage. Class and materialist politics have dominated Scottish politics. Even the SNP, which at first sight might be thought to operate on a different dimension, is a materialist party.

The relationship between class and nationality, the key cleavages in Scottish politics since the war, has changed. It is not that nationality has become more important so much that its interaction with class has changed. For most of the post-war period, the question of Scotland's constitutional status was seen as competing with class politics for the attention of the Scottish public. From the late 1960s there was speculation that the cleavage based on nationality might replace that of class. In the 1980s and 1990s nationality and class politics complemented one another.

A dichotomy appears to have emerged in post-war Scottish politics among the public at large – if not the parties. In the early years it was largely based on class, with religion playing some part. This was reflected in support for Labour and the Conservatives. By the 1980s, the dichotomy was based on a Scottish/progressive/leftist platform versus a British/unionist/rightist platform. The SNP and Labour belong to the former and the Tories the latter. The Liberal Democrats' voters are quite diffuse though the Party's elected representatives are firmly in the former camp.

The conclusion, therefore, is that the translation from public opinion to political representation in Scotland has changed. The views of the Scots were fairly well represented in the early post-war period but increasingly the political system has failed to achieve this. This is not simply the result of the party in power having minority status, though that should never be ignored. It is a function of an electoral system and party system which has not allowed for a true expression of public opinion to be made.

What, then, has shaped Scottish politics in the post-war period? Extraneous events and structural considerations have played a dominant part. Economic conditions, international ruptures and employment patterns have all been important. Scottish politics have also been shaped by a kind of pressure-group politics writ large, with Scotland operating as a group making demands on the British Treasury. The demise of the British economy and the rise of Thatcherism have made this more difficult. They have played a significant part in sharpening the one cleavage which has grown in importance over the post-war period – that based on nationality.

Lipset and Rokkan's four cleavages are evident in Scottish politics. Religion is less a political identity in Scotland than in many other parts of Europe though more so than in England. The urban–rural divide has lost much of its previous significance. Nationality remains contentious but debates on this are conducted in a far more civilised manner than in many other parts of Europe. Class remains central to Scottish politics, as elsewhere, even if the term is now less a part of political discourse. Many of the trends and issues discussed in this chapter are also found in other parts of Europe. Overall, it is difficult to avoid the conclusion that Scotland is distinct but ultimately there is much which makes it similar to other parts of western Europe.

Part I

The parties and political context

2

Parliament, Scottish administration and local government

Politics is not simply about political parties and elections. Parliament is central to Scottish politics and procedures have evolved to cater for Scottish business. The administrative politics of Scotland must also be taken into account. Much that makes Scotland different is to be found in its system of administration and local government. Over time, Scottish central and local government have evolved to create a distinct structure of politics. Scottish party politics and the behaviour of the Scottish electorate occur in this context.

Scottish representation at Westminster

The parliament of Britain has always catered for Scottish distinctiveness. At the time of union in 1707, a quota of forty-five Scottish MPs was added to the existing House of Commons (which had 513 Members). The quota took no account of the relative populations of Scotland and England, which nobody knew anyway. Also under union settlement, it was agreed that sixteen Scottish peers would sit in the Lords. These sixteen were elected from among and by the hereditary peers of Scotland. So long as this procedure existed it provided a very limited elected element to the constitution of the Lords. The Peerage Act 1963 gave all holders of a Scottish peerage a right to membership of the House of Lords.

As in other areas, the means by which Scottish distinctiveness has been catered for has changed over time. The changes have been piecemeal and largely in response to expressions of dissatisfaction from Scotland. The major reform acts extending the franchise in England also applied to Scotland, although there were some differences in detail: in 1867 suffrage was extended to occupiers of premises in English counties valued at £12, whereas in Scotland the value was lowered only to £14. However, the general trend was the same. Franchise extension also saw Scotland's share of seats in the Commons increase. Under the 1832 Reform Act, Scotland was apportioned eight new seats, giving a total of fifty-three. Under the 1867 Reform Act, seven additional seats gave it a total of sixty. Under the third Reform Act (1884/5), a more accurate account of the Scottish population was reflected in the Commons, with seventy-two seats for Scotland out of a total of 670. The number of Scottish MPs rose to seventy-four by the end of the century, but fell to seventy-one after the Second World War with the abolition of university seats. In 1983, the number rose to seventy-two following a boundary review.

The twentieth century has seen Scotland's relative share of the British population fall, but the number of Scottish MPs has remained largely unaltered. Since the union, Scotland has been both under- and over-represented, as measured by share of population. The current over-representation is generally justified on three grounds: first, Scotland's distance from Westminster; second, the preponderance of very large, rural constituencies (with 9 per cent of Britain's population, Scotland has 32 per cent of its land mass); and third, recognition that Scotland has a distinct status within Britain. The only rule applying to the Scottish Boundary Commission, which is separate from that for England and Wales, is that there must be a minimum of seventy-one constituencies in Scotland. It should also be noted that the recent growth in the size of the Commons, with eight more MPs after 1997, occurred because the English Boundary Commission regarded maintaining the existing number of seats as a desirable objective rather than as a clear objective, as the Scottish Commission did. In this respect at least, as Curtice has argued, Scotland's pattern of representation in the Commons is a 'model to be emulated rather than criticized' (Curtice 1996: 250).

Parliamentary procedure and Scottish interests

In the Commons, special procedures have evolved for dealing with Scottish business. The House of Commons established a Scottish Standing Committee on an experimental basis in 1894, which consisted of all the Members representing Scottish constituencies, together with fifteen other Members. The fifteen others were to be selected with regard to the 'approximation of the balance of parties in the committee to that of the whole House' (Sessional Order 4, Par. Deb. 23, c. 1613). The reference to parties in the sessional orders establishing this Scottish Standing Committee was unique. Parties were not normally acknowledged to exist in the formal proceedings of parliament. The Conservatives ended the experiment after they came to power in 1895 but it was re-established in 1907 by the Liberal government and has since become a permanent feature of the Commons.

The functions and powers of the newly established Committee have changed over time. The re-established Committee in 1907 had wider powers than its predecessor; not only would it consider government bills referred to standing committees which related exclusively to Scotland, but it was to be convened for the consideration of all public bills relating to Scotland. The determination of whether a bill was exclusively Scottish or not was to be decided by a ruling of the Speaker. The criticism often made that it was not Scottish, not grand and not really a parliamentary committee concerned its limited powers and the number of added members of the Committee who did not represent Scottish constituencies. In February 1919, an amendment to standing orders altered the number of added members to between ten and fifteen.

Increases in the powers of the Scottish Grand Committee occurred after the Second World War, in response to agitation for home rule and to tackle parliamentary congestion. In January 1948, the Labour government proposed that Scottish estimates (public expenditure), or a part of them, should be referred to the Committee. A further concession was to allow second readings of Scottish bills to take place in the Scottish Grand Committee. Three categories of bills were seen as appropriate for referral: technical bills applying only to Scotland; bills for Scotland which either were already enacted or were proposed for England and Wales; and Scottish bills for which time could not be found.

In essence, if a Scottish bill was discussed by the Scottish Grand Committee it was deemed to have received its second reading. One English Conservative who had opposed the changes described them as 'futile ... a meaningless sop to the Scottish Nationalists' (*Hansard*, Commons, vol. 450, col. 416, 28 April 1948). Significantly, these changes were made against a background of agitation in Scotland for reform fuelled by a belief that Scottish political distinctiveness was being eroded. The response of modifying parliamentary procedure may have been limited, but it was in the tradition of recognising and accepting the need to respond to Scottish grievances.

In 1957, following the recommendations of the Select Committee on Procedure, further changes to parliamentary procedure were made. A Scottish Standing Committee (standing committees give detailed consideration to legislation) was set up with a minimum of thirty MPs representing Scottish constituencies and up to twenty others to reflect party balance in the Commons. To this was devolved the Scottish Grand Committee's original function of amending Scottish bills at committee stage. The Grand Committee was to continue to debate second readings and estimates and, additionally, was to be able to debate 'matter', any business affecting Scotland, on two days each session. A second Scottish Standing Committee was set up in 1963, again initially on an experimental basis, in response to claims that

Scottish business was still being dealt with inadequately. Additionally, the Grand Committee was given powers to take the report stage of bills which had passed second reading there. The size of the Standing Committees was reduced in 1971 by the Conservative government. Having won only twenty-three seats in Scotland, it was clearly in their interest to reduce the size of the committee.

A select committee (select committees scrutinise government departments and conduct enquiries) on Scottish affairs was set up as part of a package of reforms in the late 1960s under a Labour government. The concerns of the committee were broadly defined to include not only the activities of the Scottish Office but all government business in Scotland. Despite its lack of Scottish MPs, the Heath government decided to reconstitute the committee in May 1971. Two enquiries were conducted, one on economic planning and the other on land-use policy (the first committee had sixteen members, the second had fourteen). The committee was not re-established during that parliament though the Heath government had indicated its intention to do so in 1973/4. There was no major change in parliamentary procedure affecting Scotland in the late 1970s though a great deal of parliamentary time was devoted to debating devolution.

Developments in parliament since 1979

The next major set of changes came after the return of the Conservatives in 1979. The background to these changes were proposals made by the Select Committee on Procedure in 1978 and the devolution debate of the late 1970s. A series of new select committees were established, including one dealing with Scottish affairs. Changes were also introduced to the Scottish Grand Committee. It was no longer to have any additional members: it would consist only of all MPs with Scottish constituencies. The removal of the additional members was not particularly radical. Under the terms of the rules which had applied with up to fifteen added members, the Conservatives would still not have enjoyed a majority on the Scottish Grand Committee. Fifty added members would have been required in 1979 to give the Conservatives an overall majority on the Committee (sixty-two after the 1992 election). If anything, the decision to abandon having added members exposed the weakness of the Committee.

It was to be permitted to meet occasionally in Edinburgh and given more days to debate 'matter'. The decision to hold meetings in Edinburgh on an experimental basis was a symbolic gesture proposed by Peter Fraser, a newly elected Scottish Conservative MP. The meetings were to take place in the old Royal High School, which had been scheduled as the venue for the Scottish Assembly proposed by the Labour government. The Scottish Grand Committee met on twenty-one occasions in Edinburgh between its first meeting in February 1982 and June 1991 and discussed a wide range of subjects. Conservatives argued that it brought parliament closer to the public and allowed lobbying to take place at each meeting. The extent of public access was limited, however, as there was space for only fifty-four seats in the public gallery. The Scottish Grand Committee had become more 'Scottish' in the 1980s but it was no more influential.

The Select Committee on Scottish Affairs, with thirteen members and a quorum of five, was the largest of the select committees set up by the government in 1979. It was generally deemed to be too cumbersome, and pressure for a reduction in its size was voiced early on, particularly from the Labour benches. Debate on the chair of the Committee at its inception heard complaints from some of the government's backbenchers when it was decided that an opposition member should take the chair. In its early years, its Conservative members took the unusual step of appointing an unofficial majority leader on the Committee. This reflected the nature of the Committee as a forum for inter-party disputes in a context in which Scotland's constitutional status was unresolved rather than one which might have approached the scrutiny of Scottish affairs seriously.

The impact of the Committee's reports has been limited. The Committee frequently divided on party lines and had little impact on public policy making. This was evident with its first report, enquiring into inward investment. There is some evidence that when the Committee worked in conjunction with the Scottish Office to press other branches of central government it could maximise pressure. The Committee reached conclusions which were in part similar to those of the Scottish Office in the case for retaining Prestwick Airport. Combining with the Scottish Office and others lobbying for an agreed Scottish 'national interest' proved its most effective role.

A view developed inside the Scottish Conservative Party was that a great deal of time was being spent by their backbenchers on the work of the Select Committee. Added to this was a perception that many reports were simply attacks on the government. After the 1987 election, when the number of Scottish Conservative MPs fell to ten, the government had difficulties finding backbenchers to sit on the Committee. A proposal to reduce the size of the Scottish Affairs Select Committee from thirteen to nine, necessary to give the Tories a majority on the Committee, was still not enough. A number of Scottish Tory backbenchers refused to serve on it. A report of the Procedure Committee of the Commons in 1990 observed that the inability to appoint the Committee was 'regrettable':

> Moreover, the absence of a Scottish Affairs Committee leaves a major Government Department unscrutinised and thus constitutes a deficiency (some would consider a serious deficiency) in the departmentally-related Committee system. (House of Commons 1990)

Another Scottish feature of parliamentary procedure is the scrutiny of Scottish Office business through questions in the House of Commons. Parliamentary questions are a very British form of scrutiny. The Scottish Office ministerial team, like other departments of state, are bound to respond in oral and written form to questions from MPs from any part of Britain. A common complaint is that the infrequency of Scottish questions results in an inadequate form of scrutiny. As questions are asked on rotation to the different departments of state, Scottish Office oral questions must wait their turn in the queue. While there are no restrictions on the number of written questions that can be asked, it is the oral sessions which gain greatest media coverage. Even assuming that question time could be an effective means of scrutinising the executive, the wide range of responsibilities covered by the Scottish Office (see below) means that effective scrutiny of its business by parliament is difficult. The fact that Scotland's population is less than 10 per cent of that of the whole of Britain has no bearing on this. What is significant is that the Scottish Office's responsibilities cover the equivalent of about nine functional departments in Whitehall. There is clearly no equivalence in terms of parliamentary time set aside for scrutiny of its activities. A complaint frequently voiced by Scottish MPs since 1987 has been that the attendance at Scottish questions of a group of English Conservatives asking questions designed purely to engage in partisan point scoring, while entirely within the rules of the game, has further eroded the value of Scottish question time.

Taking stock

After the 1992 election, the government embarked on a 'stock-taking' exercise focusing on Scotland's status within the union. This resulted in the publication of a white paper, *Scotland in the Union: A Partnership for Good* (Cm 2225), in March 1993. Among its proposals were reforms of Scottish parliamentary business. These were agreed a year later and included occasionally having a question time for Scottish ministers in the Scottish Grand Committee and opportunities for government ministers to make statements before it. There was also to be greater scope for debates and meetings of the Committee in different parts of Scotland.

Further changes were proposed by Michael Forsyth after he became Secretary of State for Scotland in 1995. These were proposed as alternatives to devolution, which Forsyth argued would damage the Scottish economy. He proposed that Scottish bills should have their second readings in the Scottish Grand Committee 'whenever it makes sense' that that should happen. He further proposed that third readings should also take place in the Grand Committee. Debates within the Committee would not be restricted to the responsibilities of the Scottish Office and Scottish law offices. His most radical proposal was that government ministers, including the Prime Minister and Chancellor of the Exchequer, would participate in debates of the Scottish Grand Committee in Scotland, though not to vote or count towards a quorum. These were similar to the 'taking-stock' proposals, but Forsyth's presentation was more skilful.

Change in parliamentary procedure affecting Scotland has come slowly over the course of the last century. On each occasion, changes have occurred in response to Scottish grievances, usually that Scotland is being neglected, or as part of a package of other changes in parliamentary procedure, or in response to the pressure of parliamentary business. While special procedures have been developed, Scottish MPs as a group have had a fairly limited role as legislators though they have been given an increasing role in the scrutiny of Scottish business.

Evolution of 'administrative devolution'

It could be argued that the corollary of a single parliament for Britain is that administrative responsibilities among ministers would be distributed on a British basis. It might be argued, for example, that it is illogical for three ministers to share the responsibility for the Health Services – the Secretary of State for Scotland, the Secretary of State for Wales and the Secretary of State for Health in England. The office of Secretary of State for Scotland seems an anomaly and a case could be made for its abolition, but, as the Royal Commission on Scottish Affairs recognised in 1954, such an argument takes no account of the 'existence of a separate Scottish ethos, history and tradition, and of practical differences between the two countries' (Balfour 1954: para. 109). The central administration of Scotland has always been different from that of the rest of Britain. Owing to its origins in the distinctive pattern of administration at the time of union, separate local administrative arrangements and the separate legal system, the prospect of introducing a uniform structure of central administration was unlikely from the outset. As the state's functions increased this offered the possibility of centralisation, but the existing separate Scottish central administration provided a base of continuing and growing distinctiveness.

A collection of boards, appointed by patronage and based in Edinburgh, developed in the nineteenth and early twentieth centuries, had responsibility for a range of matters such as manufactures, fisheries, poor law and public health, lunacy and mental health, prisons, education and agriculture. But increasing concern that Scotland's interests were not given sufficient attention in London led to calls for a secretary of state with a seat in the cabinet to look after Scottish interests. Through the cooperation of Conservatives and Liberals this demand was partially conceded in 1885, when the office of Secretary for Scotland was established. Since 1892, this minister has been a permanent member of British cabinets, war cabinets apart, and in 1926 the largely symbolic gesture was made of upgrading the office to one of a secretary of state, as originally requested by local authorities and political parties in the nineteenth century. The Edinburgh boards did not disappear with the advent of the office, but had done so by 1939.

The Scottish Secretary's main function has always been to represent Scottish interests in cabinet and the cabinet in Scotland, but he also had administrative responsibility for a range of government activities in Scotland. Initially, the administrative functions were limited, but they have grown considerably. From having responsibility for education, though not the universities, and local government in 1885, responsibilities were added including law and order in 1887, agriculture in 1912, and health and housing in 1919. By the First World War, the Scottish Office had accumulated a wide range of responsibilities. From the doubts expressed before the establishment of the Scottish Office as to whether any clear administrative role could be found for it, it has developed a vast array of administrative duties. Robert Munro, who served as Scottish Secretary from 1916 to 1922, noted the difficulties of performing the duties involved in holding that office then, when its remit was relatively light compared with today:

> A Secretary for Scotland must put a severe curb upon his personal predilections, and endeavour to deal with those branches of his activities, whatever they may be, that call for immediate attention. He cannot, being merely human, expand habitually to the width such a catalogue would demand. He has to live from day to day, to attend Cabinets, to think of Upper Silesia as well as, let us say, Auchtermuchty. (Munro 1930: 282)

Scotland is not alone in having a territorial department with a wide range of functions and responsibilities but it was the first part of Britain to develop this system of administration. The Welsh Office was set up in 1964 and the Northern Ireland Office in 1972. There are two main reasons why the Scottish Office was set up and developed as it did. In the widest sense, Scottish nationalism played its part. British governments have felt it necessary to respond to demands to accommodate Scottish distinctiveness. The Scottish Office has been the primary response to such demands. Second, it often proved administratively convenient to administer public policy on a Scottish basis, particularly if a precedent or parallel situation prevailed in another policy area. More often, the case for the Scottish Office gaining responsibility for some function was due to a combination of these factors. In education, for example, there has been a strong sense that Scotland has a distinct educational tradition. Equally important has been the existence of a distinct Scottish administrative apparatus (McPherson and Raab 1988).

The Scottish law officers – the Solicitor-General and Lord Advocate – work closely with the Scottish Office. The Scottish Office (Table 2.1) and law officers have responsibility for the equivalent of approximately nine English functional departments: agriculture, education and science, employment, environment, health, home affairs, legal offices, trade and industry, transport. Before mergers and reorganisation within Whitehall in the late 1980s, the Scottish Office had equivalent responsibility to about eleven English departments of state.

The Scottish Office is sponsoring department for a large number of agencies and quangos. One calculation suggests that there are 374 extra-governmental agencies attached in some way to the Scottish Office, with up to 3,800 appointees. This latter figure compares with 1,245 local government councillors in Scotland. These agencies include Scottish Enterprise and Highlands and Islands Enterprise, which was set up in 1991 to replace the Scottish Development Agency (SDA) and Training Agency. The SDA, a regional development agency set up in 1975, had played a significant part in urban regeneration. The Training Agency, formerly the Manpower Services Commission, had been responsible for training. It was anticipated that the new body would coordinate the work of a network of local enterprise companies headed by local business people around Scotland.

Scottish Enterprise continued the work of its predecessors but marked a shift in approach which some commentators felt had more to do with addressing the political problems of the Conservative Party than economic development issues (Danson *et al.* 1989). A similar charge might be laid against the change in the central administration of housing. Scottish Homes replaced the Scottish Special Housing Association and the Housing Corporation in Scotland in 1989 though the role of the new body differed in important respects from that of its predecessors. Scottish Homes was charged with offering strategic direction in housing policy and implementing the government's objectives of pursuing increased home ownership, diminishing the role of public-sector landlords, facilitating an increased role for private finance in housing and revitalising the private rented sector.

This wide range of responsibilities is not the complete picture. As a department with the principal function of representing Scottish interests in government, the Scottish Office has developed a less precise but no less important role. As an official committee set up to consider central administration in Scotland noted in 1937:

> there is an increasing tendency to appeal to him [the Scottish Secretary] on all matters which have a Scottish aspect, even if on a strict view they are outside the province of his duties as statutorily defined. No view of the difficulties and the peculiarities of the office of the Secretary of State would be complete unless it realises that, even apart from his multifarious duties,

Table 2.1. Structure of Scottish Office (October 1996)

Post holder	Title	Departments	Responsibilities
Michael Forsyth MP	Secretary of State for Scotland		
Lord James Douglas-Hamilton	Minister of State	Scottish Office Home Department	Police and fire services; civil law and criminal justice; emergency planning; social work services; Scottish Prison Service; Scottish Office Pensions Agency; Scottish Courts Service
		Scottish Office Department of Health	National Health Service; health policy and public health
		Scottish Office Development Department	Building control; construction industry; roads and transport
		General Register Office (Scotland)	Scottish Records Office; registers of Scotland; Scottish courts administration Spokesman in Commons on arts and historic Scotland
Raymond Robertson MP	Under-Secretary of State, Minister for Education, Housing and Fisheries	Scottish Office Education and Industry Department	Primary, secondary, further and higher education; youth and community services; sport and recreation training; Student Awards Agency for Scotland
		Scottish Office Development Department	Housing; urban policy
		Scottish Office Agriculture, Environment and Fisheries Department	Scottish Fisheries Protection Agency; spokesman in Commons on agriculture

George Kynoch MP	Under-Secretary of State, Minister for Industry and Local Government	
	Scottish Office Education and Industry Department	Industrial and regional development; Scottish Enterprise; Highlands and Islands Enterprise; Scottish Tourist Board; coordination of government action in relation to the Highlands and Islands; energy
	Scottish Office Development Department	Local government and local government finance; town and country planning; new towns; European structural funds
	Scottish Office Agriculture, Environment and Fisheries Department	Water and sewerage
		Spokesman in Commons on forestry and the environment
Earl of Lindsay	Under-Secretary of State, Minister for Agriculture, Forestry and the Environment	
	Scottish Office Agriculture, Environment and Fisheries Department	Agriculture; pollution control; coordination of rural affairs; Scottish National Heritage; forestry; Scottish Agricultural Science Agency
	Scottish Office Education and Industry Department	The arts; museums and libraries; Scottish Arts Council
	Scottish Office Development Department	Historic Scotland
		Spokesman in the Lords on all Scottish affairs

there is a wide and undefined area in which he is expected to be the mouthpiece of Scottish opinion in the Cabinet and elsewhere. (HMSO 1937: p. 19, para. 37)

The committee noted that the Scottish Secretary had come to be seen as 'Scotland's Minister' (HMSO 1937: p. 19, para. 37). This is no less true today than it was sixty years ago. As press releases and statements by Scottish Office ministers testify, issues of defence and macro-economic policy as they affect Scotland are matters on which the Scottish Office is expected to express a view both for the government in Scotland and for Scotland in government. It was no doubt this which prompted Malcolm Rifkind, when Scottish Secretary, to liken the office to a colonial governor-generalship and James Kellas to refer to the Scottish Secretary as 'Scotland's Prime Minister' (Kellas 1989: 27).

Policy making, policy innovation and channels of interest

The term 'administrative devolution' implies that some measure of autonomy exists at the Scottish level. The nature and extent of this autonomy have become contentious issues in Scottish politics. Supporters of the present arrangements argue that the existence of the Scottish Office gives Scotland influence in the centre of government. They present it as a form of autonomy and implicitly suggest that Scotland has an advantage over parts of England. Supporters of constitutional change in Scotland either question the extent of this autonomy or argue that the real issue is not whether the Scottish Office has autonomy but who controls it. The Scottish Office lies at the centre of debates in other respects too. In 1885, Lord Salisbury portentously warned the first Scottish Secretary that 'measured by the expectations of the people of Scotland' the Secretaryship for Scotland was 'approaching the Arch-angelic' (Hanham 1965: 229). It is the focus of pressure-group and party-political activity. Whenever a factory is closing or a road is to be built, local communities petition the Scottish Office and Scottish Office ministers are expected to do what they can to defend Scottish interests.

A key question concerns the degree of autonomy of the Scottish central administration. The answer is determined by a series of considerations. If distinctive Scottish circumstances already prevail, it is more likely that innovation will occur. However, it is unlikely that any completely different course would be permitted in Scotland and certainly not if it challenged British ideological cohesion. Another consideration is that of 'spillover'. If a distinct policy is pursued in Scotland it may give rise to calls for similar treatment in England. The greater the likelihood of calls for similar treatment, the less likely the chances of Scottish policy innovation, even if this means ignoring the wishes of the Scottish electorate. Closely related to this is the most important constraint on the Scottish central administration – finance. Any new policy may be judged not simply by its Scottish costs but by the implications of its extension to the rest of Britain. Consequently, the Scottish Office tends to follow English functional departments rather than lead in policy innovation. The Scottish Office budget is largely derived by a formula, which severely limits its autonomy, though the Scottish Secretary has autonomy to decide how the money is spent.

On the other hand, the Scottish Office can be responsive to Scottish demands. The idea of a 'Scottish political community' is a vague and highly contested notion. However, if a wide range of interests including the political parties, pressure groups, media and, most importantly, the party in power can reach agreement on an issue, there is a possibility that Scotland will be able to 'go its own way'. This occurs when the Scottish Office acts as a kind of institutional pressure group for Scottish national interests within government. Occasions when this has occurred tend to be defensive rather than innovative, such as the campaign in the early 1980s to save Ravenscraig steel mill. Later campaigns failed, despite the probability that a majority of Scots would have supported saving the steel industry, largely because of divisions within Scotland and, in particular, the governing party's opposition to taking action.

The Scottish central administration offers possibilities under unusual conditions for the defence of what may be perceived in Scotland to be 'national interests' but rare occasions for the development of innovative policies without the consent of the major political actors in London. That it has been described as 'administrative devolution' has given an impression of greater autonomy and prospects for innovation than actually exist.

Scottish Office ministers

Though the Office has not been noted for its willingness or ability to innovate, the power of a single minister over the range of responsibilities is immense. A situation has arisen whereby one man (none of the thirty-four Scottish Secretaries since the Office's establishment has been a woman) has little autonomy to introduce new measures but considerable powers to block change. The addition of a junior minister after the First World War had helped lighten the duties of the Scottish Secretary but at a time when the responsibilities were increasing. Further junior ministers were added in 1940 and 1952. A minister of state was created in 1951 and since then the practice has been to have a minister of state in the House of Lords.

By convention, the Scottish Office ministerial team is largely chosen from the governing party's Scottish representation in the Commons. Scottish Lords were often appointed Scottish Secretary in the early years of its existence and one of the junior ministers is always appointed from the Lords to answer questions there and guide legislation through the upper house. The extension of the franchise after the First World War and consequent increased importance accorded to the House of Commons has meant that after the office was upgraded to a secretary *of state* in 1926 all the political heads of the Scottish Office have been members of the Commons, with a brief exception under Churchill's caretaker Conservative government in 1945. In addition to the Secretary of State, three or so junior Scottish Office ministers are drawn from the Commons. With the exception of those in the Lords, all Scottish Office ministers have represented Scottish constituencies. This has not been the case with either the Welsh Office or the Northern Ireland Office – since 1987 Welsh Secretaries have all had English constituencies (Peter Walker, 1987–90; David Hunt, 1990–3; John Redwood, 1993–5; William Hague, from 1995) and at no time since its establishment has the Northern Ireland Office had a minister from a constituency in the province.

Both Labour and the Conservatives have played the 'Scottish card' when in opposition, questioning whether the governing party is doing enough to protect Scottish interests. This is most effectively argued when the Scottish Office has been controlled by a party with minority status in Scotland. In the post-war years this occurred in 1959–64, 1970–4 and since 1979 under the Conservatives. The period since 1979 has been most significant in this respect. Constitutionally, there is no obligation on the party in government to have a majority in Scotland but politically it can cause difficulties. The loss of eleven seats between 1983 and 1987 left the Scottish Conservatives with only ten Scottish seats. A gain of one seat in 1992 still left the party in a weak position.

The pool of talent from which to choose the Scottish Office team was reduced. The only alternative would have been to appoint Conservative MPs with seats outside Scotland. By this stage the number of Tory Scots who represented constituencies in England far outstripped the number of Scottish Tory MPs. By 1992, there were four Conservative MPs representing English seats who had formerly held Scottish seats but been defeated. Three other former Scottish Conservative MPs who had been defeated in the 1980s subsequently found themselves in the Lords, where they resumed their ministerial career in the Scottish Office. This meant that a Scottish Conservative MP had a better chance of holding ministerial office than did any other group of MPs. On the other hand, a talented Scottish Conservative MP was in danger of being stuck indefinitely at the Scottish Office, with little prospect of promotion for lack of a replacement.

The impact on public opinion is difficult to detect but there is little doubt that the Conservatives' problems in Scotland were jumped on by the opposition parties. The view that the Conservatives had 'no Scottish mandate' was voiced after 1979 (Miller *et al.* 1981). This claim was increasingly heard, particularly after 1987. The Scottish Office had been set up in part to appease national sentiment but had become the focus of nationalist agitation. In early 1995, a junior minister resigned following a fracas with environmental protesters in Glasgow. This highlighted the problem the government had. Of its remaining Scottish backbenchers at the time, one was critically ill (and subsequently died), one was aged sixty-six and had been in parliament for sixteen years without any ministerial experience, and the other three had entered parliament only at the previous election. Appointing an able and experienced English backbencher would cause offence. Appointing one of the existing Scottish inexperienced backbenchers carried risks but this was thought less dangerous than breaking with tradition and appointing someone from outside Scotland. Being elected as a Conservative MP in Scotland may be difficult but once elected becoming a government minister is relatively easy.

Local government in Scotland

Much that is different about Scottish politics relates to local government. Its origins lie in the administration of the Church of Scotland but the process of secularisation and the increasing role of the state in Scottish society ensured that the Church's role has all but disappeared during the twentieth century. A further feature of the structure of local government's twentieth-century development has been its more systematic organisation and stronger links with the central government. A new structure of Scottish local government was enshrined in one of the most important pieces of Scottish legislation this century – the Local Government (Scotland) Act 1929. This abolished the myriad of local boards and councils which previously had existed and replaced them with a simplified structure consisting of:

*   4 counties of cities
*   33 county councils
*   21 large burghs
*   176 small burghs
*   196 districts

These remained in place with some alterations for over forty years but during this time pressures mounted for a further overhaul of the structure. The development of the welfare state after 1945 put considerable administrative and financial strain on local authorities, which played an important part in implementing welfare policies. The post-war period was also the period of planning, including economic and strategic planning. A growing economy and optimistic expectations of future trends encouraged the view that the structure inherited from 1929 was unsuitable for modern Scotland.

There was a degree of bipartisan consensus on the need for reform and the desire for a two-tier system of local government. The Conservative government issued a white paper in 1963 arguing for this and the Labour government established a Royal Commission on Scottish Local Government, under Lord Wheatley, in 1966. Wheatley reported in 1969, recommending a two-tier structure. Following the general election of 1970 it was left to the Conservatives to act on this advice.

Wheatley (1969) had outlined four objectives for local government:

- *power* – local government should play a more important role in governing Scotland
- *effectiveness* – it should be equipped to provide services in the most satisfactory way
- *local democracy* – power should be exercised through elected representatives
- *local involvement* – the people should be brought into decision making as much as possible

The best means of achieving these goals was through a two-tier system with certain functions operating at the regional level and others at the district level. It was felt that larger (regional) authorities were needed to deliver certain services effectively while smaller, more local (district) authorities were needed for other services and to ensure that local government was not too remote. All the existing authorities should be abolished and a new structure introduced. Wheatley's proposals involved the bulk of the most important functions being performed at regional level. Seven regions and thirty-seven districts were proposed.

The resulting legislation, the Local Government (Scotland) Act 1973, involved a major overhaul of the system and to a large extent followed Wheatley's recommendations. In the event, nine regions were set up and fifty-three districts with three all-purpose island authorities in Orkney, Shetland and the Western Isles. Whereas Wheatley had recommended that housing should be a regional function, it was decided that the district should be responsible for it. In parliament there was some debate on this point and with reference to some of the boundaries of the new local authorities. There was a sense in the Labour Party that the Conservatives had not given housing to the regions because they feared that they would predominantly be Labour controlled, especially Strathclyde Region, and would implement the Labour housing policy of low rents subsidised by rates (local property tax); that is, middle-class, Conservative-inclined home owners would subsidise the more working-class council-house dwellers. Giving housing to the districts ensured that the pockets of Conservative support in Strathclyde would be able to avoid such a policy.

The new structure came into being in the mid-1970s, a time of rising unemployment and high inflation. It was not popular, especially in Strathclyde Region, covering the Greater Glasgow conurbation and extending down to Ayrshire and northwards to include Argyll. The economic climate of the time and cuts in public expenditure, hitting local government hard, made for a difficult settling-in period for the new authorities. In 1981 an enquiry headed by Lord Stodart proposed minor changes in the structure. Far more fundamental have been the changes in the relationship between central and local government over the period from reform in the mid-1970s. Local government expenditure had been doubled in real terms between 1964 and 1975, largely through central grants to local authorities. By 1975/6, central grants to the local authorities had reached 75 per cent of local authority expenditure. By 1978/9 this had fallen to 68.5 per cent and the process of central withdrawal of support continued thereafter. By 1990/1 it had fallen to 55.3 per cent.

During the 1980s, central–local relations became the battleground for some of the most bitter political disputes in Scottish politics. As the Conservatives increasingly lost ground in local government and relied on control of local government through the Scottish Office, the party-political battle appeared to be played out between the different levels of government in Scotland – local government, directly elected by the Scottish public, and the Scottish Office, gaining its authority from parliament as a whole. A succession of legislation in the 1980s reduced the powers of local government.

The reorganisation of Scottish local government

When the Conservatives embarked on local government reorganisation in the late 1980s it looked initially as if they would be able to tap into a popular measure. The two-tier structure and large regions were thought to be unpopular and each of the opposition parties had decided that one tier should be removed in the context of establishing a Scottish parliament. However, in time what had seemed a popular measure proved highly unpopular. A poll conducted in 1991 for the Scottish Local Government Information Unit, a body supplying information for and to local government, showed that 44 per cent of respondents wanted to retain the existing two-tier structure and only 37 per cent were in favour of single-tier authorities (19 per cent expressed no preference) (Scottish Local Government Information Unit 1991). It was as if the idea had lost its popularity because it had been proposed by the Conservatives.

Consultation on the reorganisation was limited, especially compared with the previous overhaul of local government. A consultation paper was issued in June 1991 which was followed by an outline set of proposals in July

1993 and more detailed proposals in October 1992. The Local Government Etc. (Scotland) Act received the royal assent in November 1994. The previous reorganisation had begun with a white paper in 1963, followed by a Royal Commission, appointed in 1966 and reporting in 1969, and legislation which finally passed through parliament in 1973. Unlike in England there was no independent commission to make recommendations on the boundaries of the new Scottish local authorities, leading to charges from the opposition that the Conservatives were seeking to gerrymander the results of the elections to the new authorities.

The reorganisation swept away the two-tier structure, and twenty-nine unitary authorities plus the three existing island authorities took its place. The new authorities range in size from Glasgow with a population of over 620,000 to Clackmannan with under 50,000, though the three island councils are smaller, including Orkney with under 20,000 people. Elections to the new councils were held in April 1995 (Table 2.2). These proved disastrous for the Conservatives. Despite accusations that the Conservatives had gerrymandered the boundaries, the party failed to win control of a single local authority. The old authorities continued to exist alongside the new ones until March 1996, when the district and regional councils were abolished.

The introduction of single-tier local government has important implications for electoral politics. Previously, anyone employed by a regional council could stand for the district council, or vice versa. Now, around 280,000 local authority employees are prohibited from standing for election to local government.

Further controversy surrounded the future of water and sewerage. Water had been a responsibility of regional councils, but under the government's proposals these functions were to be removed from local government and handed over to three new water and sewerage authorities (East, West and North of Scotland Water Authorities) appointed by the Scottish Secretary. Apart from opposition to the removal of these functions from the control of directly elected local councillors there were fears that this was a prelude to water privatisation, as had already occurred in England and Wales.

While the reorganisation was concerned primarily with the structure of local government it has had consequences for the delivery of services. Given the need for large authorities for some services, such as education, transport and EU matters, there will be a need for joint boards. In essence, in such cases the two-tier structure will continue to exist, though there may be difficulties in reaching agreement across authorities. To ensure that joint boards are established where necessary, the Scottish Secretary is empowered to force councils to form joint boards.

The reorganisation of local government cannot be seen in isolation but is part of a long-term trend which has seen local government losing power

Table 2.2. Unitary local authority election results, 1995: number of councillors (% of vote)[1]

Council	Labour	SNP	Liberal Democrats	Conservatives
Aberdeen	30 (42.0)	1 (18.1)	10 (23.9)	9 (14.4)
Aberdeenshire	0 (6.3)	15 (33.1)	15 (24.0)	4 (10.8)
Angus	0 (15.5)	21 (53.4)	2 (6.9)	2 (18.6)
Argyll and Bute	2 (10.0)	4 (12.5)	3 (14.0)	3 (13.0)
Borders	2 (3.3)	8 (18.9)	15 (24.0)	3 (14.8)
Clackmannan	8 (54.1)	3 (38.5)	0 (3.9)	1 (3.0)
Dumbarton and Clydebank	14 (50.5)	7 (42.6)	0 (0.3)	0 (1.2)
Dumfries and Galloway	21 (25.2)	9 (14.7)	10 (10.9)	2 (10.2)
Dundee	28 (53.7)	3 (25.2)	0 (2.5)	4 (13.8)
East Ayrshire	22 (56.4)	8 (36.1)	0 (0.3)	0 (6.9)
East Dunbartonshire	15 (40.8)	0 (16.1)	9 (23.8)	2 (19.3)
East Lothian	15 (56.0)	0 (16.9)	0 (6.4)	3 (18.9)
East Renfrewshire	8 (31.4)	0 (17.7)	2 (14.9)	9 (29.2)
Edinburgh	34 (40.7)	0 (17.3)	10 (18.1)	14 (23.3)
Falkirk	23 (52.0)	8 (36.6)	0 (0.1)	2 (3.6)
Fife	54 (46.5)	9 (21.2)	25 (20.1)	0 (5.8)
Glasgow	77 (61.5)	1 (22.8)	1 (3.4)	3 (6.6)
Highlands	7 (12.2)	9 (17.4)	6 (6.7)	1 (0.9)
Inverclyde	14 (49.6)	0 (16.2)	5 (29.6)	1 (3.7)
Midlothian	13 (57.4)	2 (34.5)	0 (3.5)	0 (4.2)
Moray	3 (19.7)	13 (50.2)	0 (8.1)	0 (2.2)
North Ayrshire	27 (55.9)	1 (24.8)	0 (2.8)	1 (11.8)
North Lanarkshire	60 (62.3)	7 (30.2)	0 (0.2)	0 (3.9)
Perth and Kinross	6 (14.3)	18 (41.0)	5 (13.0)	2 (24.8)
Renfrewshire	20 (46.3)	13 (38.6)	3 (5.9)	2 (7.8)
South Ayrshire	21 (56.0)	0 (12.0)	0 (0)	4 (28.3)
South Lanarkshire	62 (57.0)	8 (26.8)	2 (7.1)	2 (7.0)
Stirling	13 (49.1)	2 (18.9)	0 (4.6)	7 (25.4)
West Lothian	15 (46.9)	11 (44.6)	0 (2.0)	1 (4.2)
Total	614 (43.8)	181 (26.2)	123 (9.7)	82 (11.3)

1. Rows do not add up to 100 per cent as independents/others are not included in the table.

to the Scottish Office. In itself this has raised questions about democratic legitimacy. The financial powers of local government have been whittled away and the imposition of rules forcing authorities to allow outside firms to tender competitively for council work add up to a much reduced role in the life of Scottish society for local government than was the case twenty years ago.

Conclusion

Since the Treaty of Union in 1707, there have been special institutional arrangements to cater for Scotland. Initially this focused on local institutions but as the state at the centre gained functions and responsibilities so pressure built up to provide special parliamentary procedures and also central administrative arrangements. Over time these have changed but certain key principles have been maintained. While Scottish distinctiveness has been acknowledged in the governance of Scotland this has been within the context of parliamentary sovereignty. Local government has been the 'creature of statute'. It has been reformed and reorganised at various stages this century. Over the last twenty years there has been a reduction in its powers as central government has taken on more powers. Central government, of course, is a slightly ambiguous notion in Scotland. It is as likely to refer to the Scottish Office as any of the other departments in London. This territorial department has been retained and its functions have grown over the post-war period. It is responsible to parliament as a whole, though reforms in parliamentary procedure have established special sessions when Scottish Office ministers are accountable to Scottish MPs. Though Margaret Thatcher felt the Scottish Office created many problems, there has been no attempt or serious proposal to abolish it. One consequence of having these peculiarly Scottish institutions is that public debates occur within a Scottish context. This has played a significant part in ensuring that a distinct Scottish politics exists.

3

The Scottish Labour Party

Historical overview

The origins of the Scottish Labour Party (SLP) date back to April 1888 when Keir Hardie contested the Mid-Lanark by-election as an independent Labour candidate. His platform in that election included home rule. But most significant was the fact that Hardie stood as an independent Labour candidate, breaking with the Liberal Party, of which he had previously been a member. Hardie and his supporters had come to the conclusion that the only way in which working-class interests could be represented politically was directly through the establishment of a new political party rather than by operating through an existing one.

A radical political tradition existed in Scotland for the Labour Party to tap into. Highland radicalism was at least as potent a force as that which was to be found in urban Scotland. Even before the establishment of the SLP, an independent Crofters' Party was established which successfully contested a number of seats in the 1885 general election (Crowley 1956). The main aim of Hardie and his immediate successors was to win representation of Scottish working-class interests in parliament. Their growing disillusionment with the 'Lib–Lab' arrangement, whereby trade unionists and radicals were represented within the Liberal Party, led to the establishment of the SLP. Within months of the by-election, the SLP was formed and its inaugural conference was held in August that year.

In 1892, the Trades Union Congress met in Glasgow and called for independent working-class representation in parliament. The following January a conference was held in Bradford which established the Independent Labour Party (ILP). The SLP continued to exist separately until 1894 when it merged with the ILP. However, in 1897 the breakaway Scottish Trades Union Congress (STUC) was formed and two years later it called for Scottish cooperation to win working-class representation; this led to the formation of the Scottish Workers' Representation Committee, which adopted the name Scottish Labour Party in 1906.

In 1909 the Scottish Workers' Representation Committee was wound up and Labour in Scotland became part of the wider British Labour Party and movement. By the time the Labour Party drew up its 1918 constitution, Scottish Labour was firmly part of British Labour, and in terms of its formal constitution the Party had only a 'regional council' in Scotland. The terminology in the Party's constitution suggested that it barely existed as a distinct Scottish force in Labour Party politics but was only a region, comparable with English regional councils. Informally, however, the Party was often referred to as the Scottish Labour Party, as if it were a separate entity from the British Party. In reality, however, a degree of informal autonomy developed. Whatever the formal constitution laid down, the Party in Scotland has at certain times acted as a fairly autonomous body. This tension between the formal and informal constitutions of Scottish Labour resembles what is found in the constitution of the state itself.

The early history of the Party witnessed a tension which has re-emerged in recent times. The relationship between Scottish and British Labour and allied organisations was not, however, a major problem for much of the twentieth century. The nationalist element within the Labour Party in Scotland was vocal in the inter-war period. A number of 'Red Clydesiders', the grouping of left-wing Labour MPs elected in 1922, argued for what amounted to independence. Tensions within the Labour Party in this period were less about the 'national question' than about the nature of socialism and the road to this goal. The ILP broke with Labour in 1932, following the collapse of Ramsay MacDonald's Labour government and the establishment of a 'National Government' under his premiership but dominated by Conservatives.

The early post-war period was a particularly British phase in politics. Labour was committed to a British welfare state and central management of the economy. The Labour Party in Scotland had a strong Scottish accent but it spoke the same language as the Party in England. Keating's analysis of Scottish MPs between 1945 and 1970 confirmed that Scottish Conservative and Labour MPs conformed more to the popular stereotype than their colleagues in England and Wales in that 'Conservative members share a more strongly upper-class background and Labour members tend towards a more strongly working-class background' (Keating 1975: 147). Scottish Labour politics was deeply imbued with working-class culture.

The importance of Scotland to Labour cannot be understated. Without Scotland, Labour would have won only two elections (1945 and 1966) since its foundation. Labour's landslide victory in 1945 followed the war and was the first general election for a decade. Labour's victory in 1966 came two years after Labour narrowly won in Britain; the 1964 victory had given

Prime Minister Harold Wilson the opportunity to use his incumbency to build support and call for an election at the most advantageous time. But Labour's apparent dominance of Scottish politics owes much to an electoral system which particularly skews outcomes in favour of the party winning the largest share of the vote when there are a number of parties in the contest. Labour's dominance of Scottish electoral politics could only be described as hegemonic in a limited sense of the word. Nonetheless, under the existing electoral arrangements, Labour has maximised its share of elected offices efficiently.

Labour has no official Scottish leader though the Secretary of State for Scotland when Labour is in power, and shadow Secretary of State, when in opposition, effectively assume this role. The Scottish Secretary is appointed by the Prime Minister. The shadow post is appointed by the leader of the opposition, though the Parliamentary Labour Party (PLP) elects members to the shadow cabinet and it is from these members that Labour's leader chooses a team of shadow ministers. Willie Adamson, a former miner, was the first Labour Scottish Secretary, in 1924, and again in 1929–31 (Table 3.1). During the war, Tom Johnston served under Churchill in the wartime coalition government and gained a reputation as one of the most successful Scottish Secretaries. He decided to stand down from parliament at the 1945 election and the Scottish Secretaries in Attlee's Labour governments were Joe Westwood, Arthur Woodburn and Hector McNeil. None of these left their mark on Scottish politics to the same extent as Willie Ross, who served under Harold Wilson from 1964 to 1970 and again from 1974 to 1976. Ross was one of the longest-serving Scottish Secretaries in the history of the office. He was a former schoolmaster who was often thought to have brought strict moralistic Scottish Presbyterianism from the classroom into Scottish Labour politics. His relationship with Wilson was close and he was given more autonomy in dealing with Scottish affairs, often to the irritation of cabinet colleagues, than any other post-war Secretary of State for Scotland. Bruce Millan succeeded Ross when Jim Callaghan became Prime Minister and was Secretary of State when devolution legislation went through the Commons.

Since Labour's defeat in 1979, there have been four shadow Scottish Secretaries: Bruce Millan, Donald Dewar, Tom Clarke and George Robertson. Millan continued in the role of shadow Scottish Secretary after the election defeat. Dewar was shadow Scottish Secretary from 1983 until 1992. He was succeeded briefly by Tom Clarke before George Robertson was given the job. In opposition since 1979, the post has involved balancing the Party's expectations, fuelled by Scottish electoral successes, meeting an SNP challenge, maintaining Party unity and maintaining the link with the Party in Britain as a whole. Successive British election defeats, combined with successive impressive performances of the Party in Scotland, have made

Table 3.1. Labour Secretaries of State for Scotland

	Years in office
William Adamson	1924, 1929–31
Tom Johnston	1941–5
Joe Westwood	1945–7
Arthur Woodburn	1947–50
Hector McNeil	1950–1
William Ross	1964–70, 1974–6
Bruce Millan	1976–9

these tasks increasingly difficult. The Labour shadow Secretary of State for Scotland is as much the Labour leader's man in Scotland as Scottish Labour's man in the shadow cabinet.

Organisation and structure

In 1994, Labour's Scottish conference voted to change the Party's name. The Scottish Council of the Labour Party – the cumbersome, and rarely used, official designation – was changed to the Scottish Labour Party. Supporters of the change referred back to the original SLP founded by Keir Hardie and maintained that Scottish Labour was, effectively, Scotland's national party and that this should be clear in its title. Opponents made reference to the Scottish Labour Party founded by Jim Sillars which broke away from the Labour Party in 1975. The change of name was symbolic but little else changed. No greater formal autonomy was won for the Party though many within the Party had been arguing for this.

As noted above, Labour has a highly centralised constitution. Informally, however, Scottish Labour has had a fair degree of autonomy. Staff in Keir Hardie House, its Scottish headquarters, are appointed by London but Scottish views are taken into account. Jack McConnell, the current general secretary of the Scottish Labour Party, was a fairly controversial appointment. He had been a member of Scottish Labour Action (SLA), a home-rule pressure group within the party (see below), though he soon became a London loyalist and abandoned his erstwhile radicalism. The London leadership is conscious of the need to take account of the strength of nationalist feeling within the Party in Scotland.

This mixture of formal and informal arrangements is important in understanding Scottish Labour. John Smith House, Labour's London headquarters, has left much to the discretion of the Party in Scotland. In the 1980s, Scottish Labour appeared to present few problems. In the 1990s, it has begun to cause the leadership some problems. Demands for greater autonomy have intensified, especially after the formation of SLA. The Monklands by-election in 1994 demonstrated that Scottish local authorities could embarrass the Party just as much, though for quite different reasons, as the so-called 'loony left' councils in London had in the 1980s. Control of the Labour Party has been more centralised under the leadership of Tony Blair than under any of his predecessors. The U-turn on devolution in summer 1996 (see below) suggests that problems in the relationship between London and Scotland are likely to arise in the future.

The SLP has rarely had a membership to match its electoral support, especially compared with the Party in England. In recent years, membership under Tony Blair has increased throughout Britain but the Scottish membership figures are not as good as might be expected. At the end of 1995, the Party in Scotland had 28,466 members compared with a British membership of 363,460. Scottish Labour constitutes 18 per cent of the PLP but only 8 per cent of Labour's membership. However, Scotland delivers just under 10 per cent of Labour's vote. The apparent mismatch between Scottish members of the PLP and Party membership occurs because of the electoral system.

Trade unions have been the backbone of Labour's organisation. They have provided not only the finance but the personnel to fight elections. Changes in the Party in recent years have resulted in the downgrading of the unions. The emphasis has increasingly been placed on ordinary Party members and, at British level at least, large financial donations from corporate and individual supporters have helped the Party. The new era into which Labour Party politics is emerging is one in which it is more truly a mass party.

Electoral performance

Labour has not achieved the dominance of Scottish politics that the nineteenth-century Liberals did but in some respects Labour's achievement is more impressive. The modern electorate is far larger and Labour faces far more competition for the vote than did the Liberals in nineteenth-century Scotland. Labour's position has strengthened over the post-war period, particularly since 1959. In that election, there was a British-wide swing to the Conservatives while Scotland recorded a swing to Labour.

Between 1945 and 1966, the age of two-party politics, Labour won between 46.2 and 49.9 per cent of the popular vote in Scotland at general elections and never won fewer than thirty-five Scottish seats (see Table 3.2). Its share of the vote has fluctuated since. The two elections in 1974 saw Labour's share of the vote fall below 40 per cent though it managed to hold on to over forty seats. More than any other party in Scotland, Labour owes much to the first-past-the-post voting system. Labour was hit by the

Table 3.2. Scottish and British election results compared (% of votes)

	Conservatives	Labour	Lib./Alliance/ Lib. Dem.	SNP	Others
1945					
Britain	39.6	48.0	9.0	0.1	3.3
Scotland	41.1	47.6	5.0	1.2	5.1
1950					
Britain	43.5	46.1	9.1	0.0	1.3
Scotland	44.8	46.2	6.6	0.4	2.0
1951					
Britain	48.0	48.8	2.6	0.0	0.6
Scotland	48.6	47.9	2.7	0.3	0.5
1955					
Britain	49.7	46.4	2.7	0.0	0.2
Scotland	50.1	46.7	1.9	0.5	8.0
1959					
Britain	49.3	43.9	5.9	0.1	0.8
Scotland	47.2	46.7	4.1	0.5	0.2
1964					
Britain	43.4	44.1	11.2	0.2	0.1
Scotland	40.6	48.7	7.6	2.4	0.7
1966					
Britain	41.9	48.1	8.5	0.5	1.0
Scotland	37.7	49.9	6.8	5.0	6.0
1970					
Britain	46.4	42.9	7.5	1.0	2.2
Scotland	38.0	44.5	5.5	11.4	0.6
1974 (February)					
Britain	38.2	37.2	19.3	2.0	3.3
Scotland	32.9	36.6	8.0	21.9	0.7
1974 (October)					
Britain	35.8	39.3	18.3	3.0	0.6
Scotland	24.7	36.3	8.3	30.4	0.3
1979					
Britain	43.9	36.9	13.8	1.6	0.8
Scotland	31.4	41.5	9.0	17.3	0.1
1983					
Britain	42.4	27.6	25.4	1.1	2.9
Scotland	28.4	35.1	24.5	11.7	0.2
1987					
Britain	42.2	30.8	22.6	1.3	3.1
Scotland	24.0	42.4	19.2	14.0	0.4
1992					
Britain	41.9	34.4	17.9	2.0	3.8
Scotland	25.7	39.0	13.1	21.5	0.7

emergence of the Social Democratic Party (SDP) and the electoral alliance the SDP had with the Liberals in 1983. Labour's Scottish vote fell to 35.1 per cent but it still managed to win forty-one seats. More Labour MPs won in 1987 than in any of the post-war elections, though it won a higher share of the vote in each of the eight elections between 1945 and 1970 than it did in 1987.

Over the post-war period, Labour's share of the Scottish vote has been higher than that recorded for the Party in England in nine of the fourteen elections and once it was the same (in 1950), while the Party's share of the vote in England exceeded that in Scotland on five occasions. In the age of two-party politics, there was little difference between the levels of support for Labour in Scotland and England but this started to change in 1959 when Scotland swung to Labour. Though the proportion of Labour voters was higher in England in both 1974 elections, that can be accounted for by the rise of the SNP. The difference between the Conservatives' share of the vote in Scotland and England was much greater in these elections.

The demise of the Scottish Conservatives under Margaret Thatcher saw Labour coming to dominate Scottish parliamentary elections. In 1987, Labour won fifty seats (69 per cent of seats), its best performance, with only 42.4 per cent of the vote. In 1992, Labour fell back slightly, winning 39 per cent of the vote but holding forty-nine seats. There were only a few seats Labour could now hope to win at the next election though boundary changes made Ayr and Stirling potential gains.

Labour contested local elections from an earlier period than its rivals in Scotland and built up a strong base in urban Scotland. The rise of the SNP in the late 1960s and again in the late 1970s removed Labour from control of many local authorities, but on both occasions Labour managed to regain control after a short time. These temporary losses of power helped Labour renew itself. The period in opposition gave the Party time to recharge its batteries and replace many less able councillors.

Since the reorganisation of local government in the mid-1970s, Labour was always able to field a large number of candidates though in recent local elections the SNP managed to field more than Labour occasionally. Labour's highest share of the vote in the local elections (between 1974 and 1994) came in the district council elections in 1984, when it won 45.7 per cent of the vote. Its lowest share of the vote in these elections was in 1977, with 31.6 per cent, at the peak of SNP support (see Table 3.3). Throughout the period of two-tier local government Labour was the dominant force in Scottish local government and came to dominate the Convention of Scottish Local Authorities. The four Scottish cities – Glasgow, Edinburgh, Dundee and Aberdeen – came under Labour control, as did much of central Scotland. This involvement gave Labour a degree of experience of government unequalled in Scotland and fed into the Party's ethos.

Table 3.3. Local election results (% of vote), 1974–94

	Labour	Conservatives	SNP	Lib./Alliance/ Lib. Dem.
District council elections				
1974	38.4	26.8	12.4	5.0
1977	31.6	27.2	24.2	4.0
1980	45.4	24.1	15.5	6.2
1984	45.7	21.4	11.7	12.8
1988	42.6	19.4	21.3	8.4
1992	34.1	23.2	24.3	9.5
Regional council elections				
1974	38.5	28.6	12.6	5.1
1978	39.6	30.3	20.9	2.3
1982	37.6	25.1	13.4	18.1
1986	43.9	16.9	18.2	15.6
1990	42.7	19.6	21.8	8.7
1994	41.8	13.7	26.8	12.0

In elections to the new unitary authorities in 1995, Labour won 43.8 per cent of the vote and 614 councillors (52.9 per cent of the total). It found itself in control of twenty of the twenty-nine new authorities. In one of the other nine, Dumfries and Galloway, Labour was still the largest party group on the council. In only two new authorities – Aberdeenshire and Angus – did Labour have no councillors. In Glasgow it won seventy-seven of the eighty-three seats on the council, and consequently the main opposition then came from within the Labour group.

A low point for Labour in Scotland came in the first direct elections to the European parliament, in June 1979. Following the Conservatives' electoral triumph at the general election the previous month, Labour morale was at a low point. The Tories pipped Labour in terms of votes, winning 33.7 per cent compared with Labour's 33.0 per cent. Of the eight Scottish Euro-seats, the Tories won five, Labour only two and the SNP one. But the Tory–Labour share of seats was reversed at the next Euro-elections, in 1984, when Labour increased its share of the vote by 7.7 per cent while the Tories dropped by 8 per cent. In 1989 Labour won seven of the eight Euro-seats while the SNP held on to the Highlands and Islands. In 1994, Labour's vote fell back when it lost North-East Scotland to the SNP. As in local government, the period between 1979 and 1992 saw Labour rebuilding and consolidating its support, with the SNP replacing the Conservatives as the main electoral challenge to Labour.

Labourism, socialism and nationalism

In his doctoral thesis on the Labour Party in Scotland, Gordon Brown (the current front-bench Labour MP) noted that in 1929 the Scottish parliamentary Labour group represented the 'voice of labour, not socialism' (Brown 1981: 484). Little has changed since. The trade union movement has played a significant part in Labour Party politics. The interests of organised labour have informed Scottish Labour Party politics to a remarkable extent. Its ethos may have been labour but this did not preclude it from being socialist or radical. Indeed, the trade union movement in Scotland has often been the vanguard of radical thought and action. The STUC has been more consistent in arguing for Scottish home rule than the Labour Party. A succession of post-war STUC general secretaries, Labour or Communist Party members, have been formidable figures in Scottish Labour politics: George Middleton (1949–63), James Jack (1964–75), James Milne (1976–85), Campbell Christie (1986–). In recent years, the comment has frequently been made that the STUC, more than the Labour Party, is the political wing of the labour movement in Scotland. Christie took a more radical stance against the poll tax than the official leadership of the Labour Party and the STUC has produced considered and well received documents on Scotland's political future (for example see STUC 1987).

The relationship between socialism and Scottish nationalism has been a controversial aspect of the Party's ideology. This was explored in a study by Michael Keating and David Bleiman (1979), both then active members of the Labour Party. Different and indeed conflicting strands in Labour's ideology have been evident since its foundation and were reflected in the Keating and Bleiman study, with the former arguing for home rule and the latter against in the book's concluding chapter. This was probably a fair reflection of Scottish Labour attitudes at the time. But since then, the balance of opinion has altered.

At its inception, home rule was at the forefront of SLP politics. Keir Hardie was a member of the original Scottish Home Rule Association. In the inter-war years, the Red Clydesiders saw home rule as a way of moving more rapidly towards socialism. Some, including Jimmy Maxton, had a sentimental attachment to Scottish national identity while others, such as John Wheatley, had a coherent ideological commitment to decentralisation and home rule. The influence of the Fabians on Labour thinking was damaging to the cause of home rule. Central demand management, nationalisation and calls for uniform benefits and equality throughout the state put paid to home rule for most of the post-war period. Though Labour fought the 1945 election on a home-rule platform, its thinking and other policies precluded any prospect of home rule in Scotland. The National Health Service which was established by Attlee's Labour government was a British, not a Scottish, National Health Service. By the late 1950s, Scottish Labour dismissed home rule on 'compelling economic grounds'. Its 1958 conference rejected home rule, stating 'Scotland's problems can best be solved by socialist planning on a UK scale' (Mitchell 1996: 312).

Labour came to accept home rule and begin its process of coming to terms with Scottish nationalism only when the rise of the SNP forced it to do so. In 1974, Labour backed home rule again. The Party had never abandoned its Scottish ethos during the period when it had opposed home rule. Willie Ross, Harold Wilson's Secretary of State for Scotland, was the embodiment of post-war Scottish Labourism – socially conservative, paternalistic and distinctly Scottish. But he accepted the devolution which Wilson felt was necessary. Reluctantly at first, Scottish Labour accepted devolution but later came to embrace it.

By the late 1980s, Scottish Labour was enthusiastically and genuinely for home rule. The experience of the Thatcher government, while Labour in Scotland commanded majority support, or at least the support of by far the largest minority, forced home the need for a Scottish parliament. Scottish Labour's home-rule views were again dominant. The Party had rediscovered its roots. Hardline antidevolutionists were reluctant to speak out against home rule even if they had doubts and instead found less obvious ways of opposing a Scottish parliament. The unionist and nationalist strands still exist within the Scottish Labour Party though the former has been in retreat since 1979.

'Red Clydeside' has been an important myth in Scottish Labour Party politics. The real extent of radicalism and revolutionary fervour on Clydeside around the time of the First World War is the subject of historical dispute. What is not disputed is that the myth has played a significant part in Scottish Labour's understanding of itself. However, in the post-war period, the Scottish Party has not produced many significant left-wing thinkers. There was no Scottish equivalent on the left of Aneuran Bevan in the 1940s and 1950s but then neither was there a Scottish equivalent on the right of Tony Crosland in the 1950s. John Mackintosh was a leading Labour Party thinker in the 1970s but Wilson prevented Mackintosh ever holding ministerial office. Mackintosh was quite independent minded and almost semidetached from the PLP. He was one of only two Labour MPs to vote against the nationalisation of shipbuilding in the late 1970s. Despite this, Mackintosh's social democracy was much closer to the thinking of most post-war Scottish Labour MPs than the socialism of Jimmy Maxton, who died in 1946.

Many Scottish Labour MPs rose through the trade unions or local government. A number of graduates made their way to nearer the top of the Party. For the most part, they were on the right wing of the Party. Significantly, however, the Social Democrats attracted only a handful of

Scottish Labour politicians when it was founded. Bunty Urquhart, former assistant Scottish organiser, defected to the SDP in 1981 as did two MPs, Dickson Mabon and Robert McLennan. However, there were many more who were seen as potential converts.

Drucker (1979) distinguished between the Labour Party's doctrine and ethos. He defined doctrine as 'a more or less elaborated set of ideas about the character of social, economic and political reality' and ethos as incorporating 'sets of values which spring from the experience of the British working class' (Drucker 1979: 8–9). Labour's Scottish radicalism is an inbuilt part of its ethos but whether that translates well into its doctrine is another matter. On a number of issues on some occasions the Party in Scotland has adopted a more left-wing policy than the rest of the Labour Party, such as unilateral nuclear disarmament, but this has not tended to be the case on those matters over which the Party in Scotland has much autonomy. The unilateralism of the Scottish Labour Party could be viewed as an indulgence by the leadership in London. That would not have been the case had the Scottish Party decided to support a mass campaign of non-payment against the poll tax.

Factions and tendencies

A myriad of factions and tendencies have been evident within Labour's fraternal ranks over the years. The Labour Coordinating Committee (LCC) was set up in 1978. It came to the fore after the defeat in the 1979 general election and argued for full employment, planned re-industrialisation and increases in public expenditure, all of which would require tight import controls and leaving the EC. This was to be Labour's alternative economic strategy (AES). In pursuit of these policies, the LCC campaigned for reforms in Labour's constitution within the Campaign for Labour Party Democracy (CLPD), automatic reselection of MPs by constituency parties, an electoral college to elect the Labour leader (rather than election by members of the PLP) and control of the manifesto by the National Executive Committee. The LCC also became associated with support for the leadership aspirations of Tony Benn.

In the early 1980s it had a great deal of influence in the Scottish Labour Party. The LCC in Scotland highlighted the Scottish dimension and its members were largely supporters of home rule. Scottish LCC members argued successfully for a Scottish parliament with tax-raising powers as part of Labour's AES. Greater autonomy for the Party in Scotland, though supported by the LCC and others, never assumed the importance that other internal reforms had. The connection between the internal constitution of the Party in Scotland and winning support for change in the constitution of the state was not so well appreciated in the Scottish LCC as it had been in the LCC at the British level. Among the demands for reform in the 1980s was mandatory reselection of MPs. In the run-up to the 1983 election, a number of Scottish Labour MPs were challenged but none was rejected. Ironically, the only Scottish MP to have been deselected was Mike Watson in Glasgow Central/Govan in 1996, a former member of LCC Scotland. While LCC Scotland was active at the Scottish level, in particular in winning seats on the Scottish executive of the Labour Party, it made few inroads into Labour heartlands in local government. In councils which were won from the Tories in the early 1980s, such as Edinburgh and Stirling, LCC had some success but they made almost no impact on the politics of Glasgow.

Militant had no following in any part of Scotland comparable to that on Merseyside. In Glasgow Pollok, Militant did become a force to be reckoned with. This had been anti-poll-tax campaigner Tommy Sheridan's base before his expulsion from Labour and the foundation of Scottish Militant Labour, a party which did relatively well in local government elections in Glasgow around the time of the poll tax. Militant in Glasgow had a quite different base from Militant in Liverpool. In Glasgow, its strength lay primarily in the large housing estates such as Pollok and it had very little support in the trade unions. Ex-Militant members had brief spells of fame in Edinburgh. Alex Wood was the first leader of Edinburgh District Council after Labour won overall control in 1984 but was eventually removed by the 'soft left'. He subsequently joined the SNP. Ron Brown had been a Militant member before being elected as MP for Leith in 1979. Brown was removed at the leadership's behest because he became a figure of fun rather than, as with Dave Nellist, the Militant Labour MP for Coventry, because he was a seen as a left-wing threat.

The demise of the Bennite left inside Labour occurred just as the Scottish dimension came to the fore. In August 1987, the LCC organised a conference in Edinburgh to discuss post-election strategy. Cross-party cooperation, more aggressive campaigning against the poll tax and parliamentary tactics were discussed. The Scottish executive called a conference for November. It was assumed that similar themes would be discussed. A number of Party members were disappointed that it had simply been a means of avoiding debate; a proposal to present a white paper on devolution was the only commitment made. This led to the formation of SLA in February 1988 (McLean, not dated: 42).

Scottish Labour Action campaigned for more vigorous opposition to the poll tax as well as greater autonomy for the Scottish Labour Party and in support of the scheme of home rule agreed by the Constitutional Convention (a cross-party body which met from 1989 which included representatives of Labour, Liberal Democrats, trade unions, churches, local authorities and others). Its influence within the Party has tended to wax and wane in parallel with support for the SNP. SLA argued for more robust opposition to the poll tax but was defeated on this. It failed to convince the Scottish Party that it needed autonomy to decide its own policies and appoint its own staff. Instead, greater autonomy was to await the establishment of a Scottish parliament. It was successful in the part it played, though SLA was not entirely united on this, in arguing for an alternative voting system for the Scottish parliament, which was agreed within the cross-party Constitutional Convention with the Liberal Democrats. Though SLA could not have achieved this on its own, it proved an important force in internal Labour Party politics on the issue.

Another grouping to emerge in recent years has been the Scottish Women's Caucus (SWC). It owed its origins in part to the LCC, in particular the LCC Scotland's Women's Committee. By the late 1980s, a number of prominent men in LCC Scotland had found a seat in parliament. There was an embarrassingly low number of women Labour MPs. In 1992, only three out of forty-nine Scottish Labour MPs were women. A fourth, Helen Liddell, was elected at a by-election in 1994. Under John Smith's leadership, Labour agreed in 1993 a policy of positive discrimination to tackle the under-representation of women. The policy had involved introducing all-women short lists in half their 'inheritor seats' (when a Labour MP retires) and half their 'most winnable seats' (Norris 1995). Quotas were favoured by SWC but led to a backlash from some male members of the Party, one of whom attacked the 'quota queens' in the Party. The policy was abandoned by Tony Blair. The Constitutional Convention became a focus for SWC activity. The principle of fair representation was agreed and the voting system adopted was felt to be more advantageous to women. Home rule came to be tied into the women's agenda of the Scottish Labour Party.

Tony Blair's decision to rewrite clause four of the Party's constitution provoked the establishment of another group, the Campaign for Socialism. A delegate from Glasgow Maryhill had caused a minor sensation at Labour's 1994 conference when he passionately argued against changing the Party's constitution and Scotland came to be seen as the front line in the battle over clause four. It was accepted across the Party that if the Scottish Party voted for the change then the battle would effectively be over. Much attention was therefore paid to the activities of the Campaign for Socialism in the lead up to the 1995 Scottish Labour conference. In the event, the Scottish conference supported the new clause four proposed by Blair.

The 1992 election campaign and after

Immediately after the 1992 election, Neil Kinnock stood down as Party leader. He was replaced by John Smith. Smith's background is instructive. His father had been a socialist head teacher in a remote Scottish state school. John Smith was a Glasgow university law graduate who entered parliament in 1970 for North Lanarkshire. He continued to practise law after entering parliament and became an advocate and Queen's Counsel. Scotland proved to be a solid base for Smith but one he did not wish to be tied to. He turned down an offer to be a Scottish law officer in Harold Wilson's Labour government in 1974. He argued against Scottish devolution in the early 1970s but came to be the minister at the Privy Council office between 1976 and 1978 charged with devolution. As shadow Employment Secretary between 1983 and 1985, Smith was in charge of Labour's industrial relations policy during the miners' strike but spent more time in the law courts than playing an active part in the dispute. He had been seen as a potential convert to the SDP in the early 1980s but instead kept his head down and avoided engagement in Labour's internal debates. Solidly on the right of the Party, he was, however, a reluctant and gradual moderniser.

His brief period of leadership lasted until his death in May 1994. During this period, the leadership was criticised, from both within and outside, for being too Scottish. Smith's private office included a high proportion of Scots. This was partly due to the appointment of people Smith knew and trusted. The shadow cabinet also had a large number of Scots in it. This had little to do with Smith but arose partly because the Scottish contingent constituted almost a fifth of the PLP and included talented MPs such as Robin Cook, Gordon Brown and Donald Dewar. It was elected by the PLP as a whole.

The nationalist wing of Scottish Labour was active immediately after the election. New groupings were established. Most notable was Scotland United, a cross-party grouping which included a number of Labour MPs. In large measure, this reflected the exasperation felt by the Party in Scotland, having once more won an election in Scotland but failing in Britain as a whole. Smith's leadership was welcome to most sections of Scottish Labour. He was trusted on home rule, more so than Kinnock ever was, which Smith referred to as his 'unfinished business'. His leadership played an important part in calming the Party in Scotland. His death was to reawaken fears that the leadership in London could not be trusted.

Tony Blair's background was quite different from Smith's. Blair's father had been an aspiring Tory politician who sent his son to private schools, including Fettes, one of the most exclusive Edinburgh schools. Blair studied law at Oxford before becoming a barrister in England. This privileged background gave him little insight into the traditions and ethos of Scottish Labour. He was a fervent moderniser with few, if any, attachments to 'old Labour'. Blair has been fond of comparing himself with Margaret Thatcher. This has been an uncomfortable comparison for some in Scottish Labour. His strategy of winning over Tory voters in the south of England concerns those in Scottish Labour who believe that Labour's success in Scotland requires it to retain its 'old Labour' image. They fear that modernisation might, in time, lose the Party support in Scotland. They note that Thatcher initially inherited a policy of devolution which she diluted in opposition and abandoned in government.

Blair would be unlikely to abandon devolution but might wish to play it down during the election. His decision in the summer of 1996 to call a two-question referendum came as a surprise to Scottish Labour activists, including John McAllion, front-bench spokesman on devolution. The first question was whether Scotland should have a parliament and the second was whether the parliament should have tax-raising powers. The change of policy was designed to meet the criticism made by Michael Forsyth, Conservative Secretary of State, that Labour would introduce a 'tartan tax'. The home-rule scheme agreed by the Constitutional Convention had included limited tax-raising powers and was seen as a complete package. Blair's approach was typical of the approach he adopted on other issues. He moved on to the Conservative agenda in the hope of capturing it for Labour rather than confronting the Conservatives and offering an alternative. If the Scots wanted a tax-raising parliament they could vote for one but Labour would not be associated with this policy. Indeed, Labour could present itself as being as tough on taxes as the Tories. The blurring of the distinction between Labour and the Tories which had been evident on almost all other major issues but the constitution had not occurred here, but there was some change.

The key question for Scottish Labour is just how autonomous it will be in the future. This will depend on Scotland's constitutional status. Labour's reliance on Scotland for seats makes even a modest degree of autonomy unlikely. Labour's approach to its own constitution is quite different from its approach to the British constitution. It is feared that devolving power to the SLP might start a movement for greater autonomy. The 'slippery slope' might lead to a breakaway if Scottish Labour became disillusioned with British Labour. In the event of a Scottish parliament being established, the SLP will become more autonomous, whether formally or informally. A new relationship is most likely to develop.

4

The Scottish Conservative and Unionist Party

Historical overview

The Conservative Party in Scotland has undergone great changes in the post-war period. Its organisation, policies and ideology, base of support and even its name have all changed. Its origins lay inside parliament and the Party claims to be the oldest in Scotland. The extension of the franchise forced the Party to develop an organisation outside parliament, including north of the border. In the nineteenth century the Party fared poorly in Scotland. It was the Liberal Party which dominated Scottish politics. The conversion of the Liberal Party to the cause of Irish home rule under Gladstone in 1886 was opposed by many Liberals and split the Party. Liberal unionists, opposed to Irish home rule, broke with the Party and found a home within the Conservative Party. This link was formally established in 1912, when the Conservatives in Scotland changed the name of the Party from Conservative Party to Scottish Unionist Party and fully accommodated the Liberal unionists. In the first half of the twentieth century the Conservatives made advances in Scotland.

The Scottish Unionist Party was the official name of the Scottish Tory Party until 1965. The term 'Conservative' was avoided as it was deemed electorally damaging. 'Unionist' on the other hand allowed the Party to appear distinct from the Party south of the border and to appeal to a sizeable section of the working-class Protestant community who identified themselves with co-religionists in Ireland and opposed Irish home rule. The unionist label also signalled opposition to Irish Catholic immigration into Scotland. This proved potent in the 1930s when unemployment was high and scapegoats were sought.

After 1945, however, the unionist label began to lose its appeal. The most important reasons were the socio-economic changes which were occurring. The coalition of support was beginning to fragment even as the Party achieved its best ever election performance in Scotland in 1955. Old communities, often rooted in religious identity, were disrupted in the age of planning, new towns and new peripheral housing schemes. Employment patterns which had been sectarian were changing, especially in the recently nationalised industries. Church attendance was falling and the relative economic prosperity following the end of rationing was conducive to greater social cohesion. All this eased the integration of Irish Catholics into Scottish society and reduced the relevance of Ireland's constitutional status to Scottish politics. Pockets of support based on the old coalition still existed but they were becoming less significant.

A degree of complacency marked the Party's attitude towards these changes and some senior members who urged change found their message fell on deaf ears. Attempts to reform the Party in the late 1950s failed and it was not until 1965 that action was taken. The symbolically important name change involved adding, and giving precedence to, Conservative in the Party's title without abandoning Unionism. The Scottish Conservative and Unionist Party also determined to contest local elections under that label whereas previously candidates had stood under other labels – Progressives, Moderates or Independents. This attempt at modernisation was half-hearted and belated, but it fitted in with the changes occurring in England following the end of the old-style Conservative leadership of Sir Alec Douglas-Home. The Party may also have inadvertently created a problem for itself by adopting the name 'Conservative', making it difficult to highlight what was distinctly Scottish about it. Seawright has suggested that the adoption of the 'Unionist' label might be electorally valuable in the context of elections to a Scottish parliament (Seawright 1996).

Ted Heath was the first Conservative leader elected by the Party's MPs rather than 'emerging' through the secretive selection process which existed until 1965. He set about changing the Party, including the organisation and policies north of the border. At a time of rising political nationalism in Scotland, Heath attempted to ally his modernisation of the Party with an appeal to home-rule sentiment, while Labour in Scotland was opposed to home rule. In his grandiosely titled 'Declaration of Perth', he informed a stunned Scottish Conservative conference in 1968 that a future Conservative government would deliver a measure of home rule. Heath never delivered on his promise, but his commitment to a measure of home rule was inherited by his successor, who was otherwise hostile to the Heathite agenda. In time, Margaret Thatcher was to reverse the policy and to become the most die-hard British nationalist Prime Minister this century.

The recovery in Conservative fortunes in Scotland in 1979 appeared to suggest that the downwards trend had been reversed. This was not to be the case. Under Margaret Thatcher the Conservatives had their worst ever performance in 1987 when they won only ten of Scotland's seventy-two seats. Thatcher's personal unpopularity was, in part, to blame. According to an internal Party document following this election, she was identified as an electoral liability in Scotland, as she was perceived to be 'English and anti-Scottish' (Mitchell 1990: vii). The election of John Major as leader and Prime Minister in 1990 marked an opportunity for the Conservatives to shed some of the unpopular imagery associated with Thatcher. The 1992 election saw a slight improvement in the Party's fortunes. A seat lost at a by-election months before the general election was regained, as was one of the eleven seats lost in 1987, and the Party's share of the vote rose from 24 per cent to 25.7 per cent (see Table 3.2, p. 50).

Organisation and structure

In the late 1950s, a section of the Party in Scotland deemed its organisation to be weak and in need of an overhaul. The Scottish Unionist Party had not undergone the extensive overhaul of its organisation and candidates list after 1945 which was experienced by the Conservative Party in England. The structure established in 1912, when the Conservatives had united with the Liberal unionists, had not undergone any major change. The Party claimed to be 'independent' of the Party south of the border, and though this was an exaggeration, it had a degree of autonomy it was not to have later. As was the case in the Party in England, the Scottish Unionist Party had a voluntary and a professional organisation. Its 'voluntary' side was organised into two divisional councils, in the east and west of Scotland. This division dated back to Disraeli's time. The degree of autonomy of each division was remarkable – there was no central Scottish fund for example – and rivalry marked the relationship as much as cooperation. The professional part of the organisation did have a Scottish dimension, with workers based in the chairman's central office in Edinburgh. The chairman was appointed by the Party leader.

For 38 years, from 1922 to 1960, the Party's chief full-time official was Patrick Blair, who served as secretary in the chairman's office. Just before his retirement, Blair initiated an enquiry into organisational problems, with the strong support of a modernising element in the Party. Plans had been laid to reorganise the party before the 1964 election and the relatively poor results north of the border provided the reformers with the 'impetus to sweep aside the obstructionists and implement sweeping changes' (Warner 1988: 210). This culminated in changes proposed to the Party conference in 1965 by Sir John George, one of its most dynamic chairmen, and supported by most of its MPs. George noted that the conference that year was poorly attended, delegates were predominantly older members and debates were lacklustre. He warned the Party that it was in danger of causing the

Conservatives to lose elections. Some reformers wanted a more radical change, including a full merger with the Conservative Party in England.

The changes instituted in 1965 were controversial though few members regarded them as having caused rather than confronted the difficulties the Party faced. Organisationally, the main change involved the abolition of the eastern and western divisional councils. A stronger Scottish central office was established with five regional councils, each with an agent answerable to the Scottish chairman. A single Scottish fund was set up with a treasurer, and the chairman continued to be appointed by the Party leader. In all, the changes amounted to a greater degree of centralisation in Scotland combined with closer links with the Party in England.

Another important change instituted in 1965 was in nomenclature. An attempt had been made in 1956 to change the Party's name to 'Conservative and Unionist'. As one opponent representing the old guard remarked, 'The word "Conservative" conveys a sense of an excessive fondness for the past, a reluctance to change, and a disharmony with ideas of progress' (Urwin 1966: 157).

Supporters of changing the Party's name felt their case was even more pressing a decade later. They argued that the change of name would enable the Party to take advantage of literature and posters produced in England. Also, as television was becoming a more important means through which electors gained information about politics and as consistency across Britain was becoming more important (Butler 1993: 66), it made sense to use the same name throughout Britain.

The Party decided to give greater prominence to local government and to urge its members to contest local elections as Conservatives rather than under a variety of other names. A compromise was reached on this issue and it was agreed that the anti-socialist candidate should adopt the Conservative banner only in Labour-controlled areas. A number of councillors resisted this but a process began which resulted in the end of the Moderates and Progressives in Scottish local government, though Independents still predominate in many parts of rural Scotland. These changes were seen as part of the new modern image which the Party was trying to project under the leadership of Ted Heath.

The change in name, image and organisation brought about in 1965 amounted to a radical departure for the Party. It fitted in with the mood of the times. But the assumption that modernisation entailed the steady elimination of territorial politics proved inaccurate (Urwin 1994). Within a short period, the centralisation and homogenisation involved in these reforms proved not to be appropriate for Scottish politics. Sir John George and the reformers may have been correct in identifying the need for change but seemingly made changes of the wrong sort. There was disillusionment within the ranks of the Party, particularly in the west, with the changes and it is possible that, instead of stemming the flow of support away from the Party, they did the opposite. Unionism was distinctly Scottish and the Party was to struggle to articulate a distinctly Scottish Conservatism. It is, however, difficult to know what might have been more appropriate. Encouraging Party activists to play a role in local government was probably sensible, but it is possible that had this been encouraged under the 'Unionist' label then the Party might have achieved a better balance in its effort to maintain its strengths while responding to changes in society.

The next major change in the Party's organisation occurred under the chairmanship of Russell Fairgrieve in the late 1970s. Once more, the catalyst was electoral defeat. Margaret Thatcher appointed a committee under Fairgrieve to look again at the Party's organisation. Fairgrieve was a 'maximalist devolutionist' in debates on Scotland's constitutional status, but when it came to the Party's organisation he argued for closer ties with the Party in England. Until 1977, the Scots could attend Party conferences south of the border, but only as observers, not delegates. This anomalous situation was changed and the Party's organisation in Scotland became more integrated with that of the south. An idea which had been regarded as too radical in the early 1960s was implemented in 1977.

Electoral performance

Earlier this century the Scottish Unionist Members Committee was set up within the Conservative Party in parliament. It consisted of all Scottish MPs and it met between five and twelve times a year during the 1930s, discussing Scottish legislation and listening to deputations from a range of Scottish bodies. It continued to meet during the war, but it was in the post-war period that meetings became more regular and better organised. By the 1950s it was meeting weekly. Until then it was the only 'regional' committee of Conservative MPs, but by 1980 there were six others (Norton 1994: 115–16).

The decline in the number of Scottish Conservative MPs since 1955 has given rise to problems. The Scottish Office and Scottish parliamentary committees require a minimum number of Scottish MPs. Conservative Scottish Secretaries in the post-war period have all been Scottish MPs (Table 4.1). With the exception of a member in the Lords, the junior ministers too have been Scottish MPs. Problems arose following the 1987 election when eleven seats were lost, including those of two junior Scottish Office ministers. The Prime Minister had a reduced pool to choose from. This was exacerbated when one, Alick Buchanan-Smith, refused to serve as a minister in the Scottish Office. There is no constitutional requirement that the Scottish Office team has to consist of Scottish MPs – the Welsh Office has been headed by an English MP since 1987 – but politically it would have

Table 4.1. Conservative Scottish Office ministers since 1945

	Years in office
James Stuart	1951–7
John Maclay	1957–62
Michael Noble	1962–4
Gordon Campbell	1970–4
George Younger	1979–86
Malcolm Rifkind	1986–90
Ian Lang	1990–5
Michael Forsyth	1995–

proved troublesome for a party which had privately acknowledged that it was seen as 'English and anti-Scottish'. There was much speculation inside the Conservative Party during this period as to what should be done, especially in the event of further losses. In the event the 1992 election gave the Party a breathing space. There were also difficulties in setting up the Scottish Affairs Select Committee after 1987 (see chapter 2).

As already noted, the local government scene became more important for the Conservatives from the mid-1960s. Following reorganisation of local government in the mid-1970s they were prominent in a number of parts of Scotland. In the regional elections in 1974, they won 28.6 per cent of the vote and 112 of the 432 regional council seats in Scotland (see Table 3.3, p. 52). In 1978 the Conservatives had their best performance in regional elections when they won 136 seats. Grampian, Tayside and Lothian regions were all at some stage controlled by the Party. Almost twenty years on, in the last elections before the regional councils disappeared with the reorganisation of Scottish local government, the Conservatives managed to contest more seats than at any previous election but they won only thirty-one. In Grampian region they could only win eight out of fifty-seven seats and in Tayside four out of forty-six. By 1994 the Conservatives lay well behind Labour, the SNP and the Liberal Democrats in terms of regional council seats held. Indeed, the Liberal Democrats, lying third, had twice as many seats as the Conservatives (Bochel and Denver 1978; Denver and Bochel 1994).

At the district elections in 1974, the Conservatives won 26.8 per cent of the vote and 241 (21.7 per cent) seats. In Dundee some candidates continued to stand under the 'Progressive' banner. In five of the fifty-three districts, Conservatives were either in overall control or formed the largest group. The worst district elections for the Conservatives came in 1988. Support slumped to 19.4 per cent and the Party won only 162 seats (14 per cent). In the aftermath of the general election in 1992, the Conservatives regained ground lost in district councils. It won 204 seats (17.6 per cent) with 23.2 per cent of the vote. After 1992, the Conservatives were in overall control of four districts – Perth and Kinross, Berwickshire, Eastwood, and Kyle and Carrick.

The first elections to the new unitary authorities in 1995 were a 'catastrophe for the Conservatives' (Denver and Bochel 1995). Party morale was low and only just over half the council seats were contested by the Conservatives. They won only 11.3 per cent of the vote, their worst ever share in Scotland. They were Scotland's third party in terms of votes, behind Labour and the SNP, and fourth in terms of seats, also behind the Liberal Democrats. Perhaps most significant was that the Conservatives failed to take control of a single local authority and were the largest party only in one, East Renfrewshire. From having more than a quarter of all councillors in 1978, the Conservatives emerged from the local elections in 1995 with only 7 per cent (Denver and Bochel 1995: 39).

The first direct elections to the European parliament were in June 1979, a month after the general election. The Conservatives won five of the eight Scottish seats, with 33.7 per cent of the vote. The Conservative vote fell at each successive European election. In 1984, they held only two seats, with 25.7 per cent of the vote, and in 1989 they lost these, winning only 20.9 per cent. In 1994 they again failed to win any and saw their share of the vote fall to 14.5 per cent. In part these swings reflected what was happening throughout Britain at mid-term for the Conservative government. The absence of any Conservative representation from Scotland in the European parliament since 1989 has been a serious weakness for the Party.

Overall, the Conservatives have suffered a sharp fall in representation at every level. From local government to Europe, the Scottish Conservatives have been marginalised in Scottish electoral politics. They maintain control of much in Scotland by virtue of the English Conservative majority which gives the Party control of the Scottish Office. Increasing centralisation of power to the Scottish Office at the expense of the local authorities has only added to the perception which developed in the 1980s that the Conservatives run Scotland, but lack a democratic mandate. Both Labour and the Conservatives have 'played the Scottish card' when in opposition. In 1967, George Younger wrote that the Scottish Office was 'controlled absolutely by Scottish Ministers who are Scots MPs backed by the 71 Scottish Members of Parliament' (Mitchell 1990: 101). In reality, Conservative Scottish Office ministers have been Scottish MPs with diminishing support of Scottish MPs and the Scottish public. At times since then it has even looked as if Conservative Scottish Office ministers would have to be drawn from outside Scotland.

Conservatism and unionism

The core beliefs of the Conservative and Unionist Party are much the same as those of the Party south of the border. The differences have largely been differences of emphasis. Unionism was the preferred term for most of this century but it would be wrong to assume that the only or even the main preoccupation of the Party was with constitutional politics. The name certainly derived from the Party's support for the union with Ireland. Even after the Irish Republic was founded, the name was preferred in part because of the associations the Party had with the unionist political community in Northern Ireland, and no doubt also because it proved more electorally appealing, at least into the 1950s. But unionism came to have a socio-economic meaning. The association with Orangeism and the Party's identification with working-class issues ensured that unionism was never a free-market ideology.

Support for tradition, the established order and conservatism found their Scottish dimension in unionism. This has caused tensions within unionism. The traditional order might be at times Scottish and at others British. For the unionist, the British tradition would have priority but tensions can exist. When Scottish traditions and institutions are threatened by unionist assimilation, the Scottish Conservative has to make the choice between Scottish and British traditions. For the most part, the Scottish Tory is disposed to finding some means of expressing Scottish distinctiveness within the union. Unionism has generally not meant support for assimilation and Britain is understood as a state which accommodates its distinctive national communities.

The Empire and support for a strong Britain could be combined with support for distinct Scottish institutions. Unionists have been fond of reminding Scots of their part in the formation and development of the Scottish Office. When in opposition, unionists have attempted to embarrass Labour by playing the Scottish card. In the late 1940s, nationalisation was presented as a form of de-nationalising Scotland as, it was argued, the newly nationalised industries would remove Scottish control of Scottish industrial affairs and place them under bureaucrats in London. Unionist politicians in the early 1950s attacked the Labour Party for the number of candidates contesting Scottish seats who were English. In the 1960s, they were prominent in campaigns to save Scottish military regiments. The imperial legacy and Scotland's distinct role within it were part of the unionist tradition.

Unionism's socio-economic base was influenced by Presbyterianism of the Liberal unionist inheritance. The fact that a sizeable section of the working class was attracted to the Party ensured that the interests of this section of Scottish society found a voice within it. Though the Party was dominated by business interests and could rely to some extent on appealing on religious grounds to the working class, socio-economic issues could not be ignored. Figures such as Noel Skelton, who originally coined the phrase 'property-owning democracy' (1924), and Walter Elliot, who influenced public policy during his ministerial career in the inter-war period, articulated a broadly interventionist philosophy which shaped the Party's outlook in the post-war period.

Unionism, then, was an ideology with a politico-religious base, founded in a belief in the maintenance of the union with Ireland and later Northern Ireland, which, with its association with the Protestant working class, came also to incorporate an interventionist public policy stand. The roots of Thatcherism were not to be found in unionism. It was hardy surprising to find Margaret Thatcher bemoaning the failed Thatcherite experiment north of the border in her memoirs (Thatcher 1993: 618–24). More than any Conservative leader this century, Thatcher failed to understand the multinational nature of Britain. Her attitude directly contradicted the unionist idea that Britain consisted of distinct national communities. Those institutions which unionists would proudly identify as embodiments of their tradition were treated contemptuously by the Thatcherites. The Scottish Office, long regarded by unionists as the classic unionist institution – providing for Scottish distinctiveness within Britain – was an institution 'whose very structure added a layer of bureaucracy, standing in the way of the reforms which were paying such dividends in England' (Thatcher 1993: 619). Under Thatcher, a more assimilationist image was projected which challenged the old unionist ideology in constitutional understanding and public policy terms: Scotland was seen as a region of Britain/England and should expect no favours or distinct policies.

Factions and tendencies

Like all parties, the Scottish Conservative Party is a broad church and within the Party different tendencies exist which at times have crystallised into factions. In the 1970s the most fractious tension existed over the issue of devolution. Conservative supporters of legislative devolution found themselves at odds with their colleagues. Around this time a view began to emerge which had hardly existed before, or which had gone unnoticed, which could best be described as assimilationist, in the sense that these Conservatives would obliterate that which made Scotland distinct. The leading proponent of this view was Iain Sproat, MP for Aberdeen South from 1970 to 1983. The most prominent devolutionist was Alick Buchanan-Smith, MP in the neighbouring North Angus and Mearns constituency. The differences between these two MPs went beyond constitutional politics. Sproat was an early

Thatcherite while Buchanan-Smith was on the left of the Party and, though never a member of the Scottish Tory Reform Group, was closely associated with it.

The devolutionist–assimilationist divide became far less significant following the result of the 1979 devolution referendum and subsequent general election. As the issue of devolution receded in importance in Scottish politics it became less significant within the Party. Even as the issue returned to prominence in the late 1980s it failed to divide the Party as it had a decade before. A few devolutionists found voice again, but largely fell silent after the 1992 election. The polarisation of the Party in the 1970s had an important legacy. The middle ground disappeared and the subsequent defeat of the devolutionist position ensured the dominance of a die-hard unionist position. The premiership of Margaret Thatcher served only to emphasise this position. By the late 1980s any prospect of a policy change looked remote, at least under Thatcher's leadership.

As in England, the key tension within the Party in the 1980s was that between its 'wet' and 'dry' wings. George Younger as Secretary of State for Scotland from 1979 to 1986 was regarded as firmly on the wet wing though a Thatcher loyalist, in much the same way that Willie Whitelaw was. During his time at the Scottish Office, Conservative support slipped away, but hostility in Scotland to the government tended to be directed at Thatcher rather than Younger. His backing for the retention of the Ravenscraig steelworks in the early 1980s and semi-public threats of resignation on the issue may have placated the Scottish public, but it irritated the Party's right wing.

In February 1985, a revaluation of rates, the local property tax, in Scotland, the third in Scotland in a period when none had taken place south of the border, caused a substantial increase in the local tax demands, which particularly affected middle-class households. At that year's annual Scottish Conservative conference, the stirrings of a middle-class revolt were in evidence. With the Party faring poorly in opinion polls, the Conservatives were looking into an electoral abyss. There were major differences between Younger and Nigel Lawson, Chancellor of the Exchequer, over the extent of financial relief to cushion the effects of the revaluation. The Scottish Conservative conference met in May with rates dominating proceedings and the Party with only 17 per cent of the vote in opinion polls. Younger wanted to commit the government to replace the rates with some alternative. Only minutes before he spoke to the conference, the Prime Minister gave him permission to state that the 'status quo is not an option' (Butler *et al.* 1994: 80). The poll tax emerged as the alternative in this unusual context. A middle-class revolt provoked fear of electoral annihilation within the Conservative Party and George Younger, head of what had been described as the 'wettest department in Whitehall' (*Daily Telegraph*, 21 March 1984), had pushed for the poll tax against the wishes of Nigel Lawson, viewed as one of the leading right wingers in the cabinet.

Legislation to introduce the poll tax in Scotland was passed in the closing days of the 1983–7 parliament. While the commitment to introduce the poll tax elsewhere in Britain was contained in the Conservative manifesto, the fact that legislation was already on the statute book for Scotland ensured that the issue was more dominant in Scotland in 1987 and fed perceptions that the Conservatives treated the Scots as guinea pigs. The defeat of eleven Scottish MPs in the 1987 general election was to heighten tensions within the Party. The Party had to explain and respond to its worst performance since universal enfranchisement. The different strands of thought in the Party had different interpretations and responses. George Younger had moved to the Ministry of Defence in 1986, and was replaced by Malcolm Rifkind. Rifkind had inherited the poll tax commitment and was on the left of the Party. His relations with Forsyth were never good, especially after Thatcher appointed Forsyth Scottish Party chairman in 1989, against Rifkind's wishes. Though Rifkind appeared to adopt a Thatcherite line for a period after the 1987 election, this proved temporary and never convinced Thatcher.

The ensuing battles were fought in public (Kemp 1993). The culmination came when the old guard, including Younger and Whitelaw, urged Thatcher to remove Forsyth from Party chairmanship in Scotland. This she did, but simultaneously promoted him from Under-Secretary to Minister of State at the Scottish Office. Forsyth's eventful term ended with his removal fifteen months later and, according to Thatcher, was due to a 'combination of the Left and the traditional establishment of the Party', the same alliance which ousted her as leader a few weeks later (Thatcher 1993: 623). Within weeks John Major had been installed as Prime Minister and leader of the Conservative Party. Major had little experience of Scottish affairs and while he was Thatcher's preferred successor, it was anticipated throughout the Party that he would be more popular than she had been. He moved Rifkind to the Ministry of Transport and appointed Ian Lang to head the Scottish Office. Lang had served with Major in the whips' office in the early 1980s and had been a member of Major's campaign team during the leadership contest. At Lang's insistence, Major moved Forsyth to the Employment Department from the Scottish Office in April 1992.

Shortly after John Major became Prime Minister, there was speculation in the media that he might radically change the Party's stance on devolution. It was soon made clear to the small group of Scottish Conservative devolutionists that this would not occur. Part of the basis for the speculation was Ian Lang's appointment as Secretary of State for Scotland. Lang had been a supporter of legislative devolution in the 1970s. In 1975 he had co-authored a pamphlet in which the Party's policy at that time, in support of a measure of legislative devolution, was backed strongly and placed within the Party's long-standing tradition of support for the union state (Lang and Henderson 1975). While speculation continued through to the general election of 1992, fuelled by media expectations of further Conservative defeats, there was little evidence to back it up.

The 1992 election campaign and after

During the 1992 election campaign, John Major spoke with 'clarity and conviction' in opposing any measure of Scottish home rule. He warned that the 'United Kingdom is in danger. Wake up, my fellow countrymen! Wake up before it is too late!' (Butler and Kavanagh 1992: 130). Contrary to many expectations, the Conservatives increased their share of the vote and number of seats in Scotland, the only party to do both. There was a modest increase in support for the Conservatives in Scotland by 1.7 per cent. Given the substantial swing away from the Conservatives in Scotland in 1987 this was not such a remarkable result. But measured against media hype and the expectations of the opposition parties, the Conservatives could claim victory.

In fact, the 1992 election result offered the Scottish Conservatives breathing space. Major indicated that he would 'take stock' of the situation in Scotland after the election. The 'stock taking' exercise was an endeavour to find a Scottish dimension for government strategy. After a number of postponements, the white paper *Scotland in the Union: A Partnership for Good* was published. In language and tone it suggested that the government understood Scotland's position within the union to be distinct and that government policy had to accommodate Scottish distinctiveness. It proposed a few minor alterations in the government of Scotland (see chapter 2). It was a fairly superficial document, especially compared with previous similar documents produced by the Party. The 'taking stock' exercise had been an exercise in symbolic politics.

In the immediate aftermath of the 1992 election, the Conservatives were given a relatively favourable press in Scotland. Soon, however, the Conservatives were back on the defensive. Opinion polls in 1994 placed the Conservatives lower than at any previous period since Scottish polls started. The Scottish Office lost a number of key battles. It lost out in the public expenditure process after the 1992 election when the formula for allocating public expenditure was altered to Scotland's disadvantage. The decision to close Rosyth Dockyard in 1993 in favour of Devonport in the south of England did not help the Conservative cause and in 1994 British Gas closed its divisional headquarters in Edinburgh.

In 1995, John Major resigned as Conservative Party leader following a period when his authority was being persistently called into question. John Redwood, the Welsh Secretary of State sitting for an English constituency, stood against the Prime Minister. The only significant Scottish angle on this leadership contest was a statement from Redwood which demonstrated that he did not realise that Scotland had a separate legal system. Notably, Michael Forsyth, always thought to be a fellow Thatcherite along with Redwood, was a loyal supporter of Major during the contest. Michael Forsyth was appointed Secretary of State in July 1995, when Lang was promoted to the Trade and Industry Department, having also been loyal to the Prime Minister. Forsyth brought far greater political skills to the office than his predecessor and caused the Labour Party serious problems with its proposals for tax-raising powers for a Scottish parliament. He hammered home the argument that Labour would give Scotland the 'tartan tax'. Forsyth had reinvented himself: as Scottish Secretary he appeared more sensitive to the Scottish dimension and less abrasive in style. Whereas he had proved a divisive force as Scottish Party chairman, he became a force for unity within the Scottish Conservatives. But his problem was reversing a long-term decline in Conservative Party fortunes.

Few commentators are now willing to predict the imminent demise of the Scottish Conservatives as they did before the 1992 election but there are fewer who see any long-term prospect of the Party returning to the pre-eminent position it commanded forty years ago. A controversial theme of much Conservative thinking since 1979 has been Scotland's financial dependence on England. A more pertinent and problematic dependence for the Scottish Conservatives is the dependence the Party has on England for its continuing role in government. Sir John George's warning to the Scottish Conservatives in 1965 that they might end up being blamed by their English counterparts for a British election defeat has never looked more relevant than it does in the 1990s.

5

The Scottish National Party

Historical overview

The Scottish National Party was founded in the inter-war period, largely as a result of disillusionment within the national movement at the failure of the Labour Party and pressure groups to deliver a measure of home rule. Home-rule pressure groups, notably the Scottish Home Rule Association (SHRA), the Scottish National League (SNL) and Scottish National Movement (SNM), had campaigned unsuccessfully in the 1920s for a Scottish parliament. A constitutional convention consisting largely of Labour Party members, local authority representatives and trade unionists met in the mid to late 1920s in an attempt to agree a scheme for home rule. Its final meetings were largely concerned with questions of strategy rather than objectives: how self-government was to be achieved rather than what form it should take. This was the background to the establishment of the National Party of Scotland (NPS) in 1928. Earlier accounts of the history of the movement have given prominence to the role of John MacCormick and students at Glasgow University in its establishment (Coupland 1954; MacCormick 1955; Hanham 1969; Brand 1978) but recent research has played down the role of students and emphasised the role played by those who had been involved for longer (Finlay 1994; Mitchell 1996). All agree that disillusionment with the Labour Party and pressure-group politics was most significant in the foundation of an independent party campaigning for self-government.

Four years after the foundation of the NPS in 1928 the Scottish Self-Government Party was established, which styled itself the Scottish Party or 'Moderates'. Its supporters tended to be less hardline on the constitutional question, favouring self-government within the United Kingdom or the British Empire. It was fairly right wing and some prominent Liberals and a few Conservatives were drawn into its ranks, giving it a less radical image than the NPS. Two years later, and largely because of the efforts of MacCormick, the parties merged to form the SNP. Bringing together such a diverse group of people and having a number of colourful figures within its ranks, the SNP's early years were marked by rancour, divisions, expulsions and resignations. Apart from personality clashes, which intruded into debates to a considerable extent, the main issues dividing the Party concerned strategy. How should the Party relate to the wider home-rule movement? What should be its relations with other parties, most notably with the Labour Party? Should electoral politics be its main or only field of activity?

In the lead up to the Second World War the Party fared poorly. By the outbreak of war, it was in a parlous state. Added to its problems was the divisive issue of war itself. Some in the Party wanted to support the wartime efforts and noted that the war was being fought in defence of self-government for small European states. Others viewed the declaration of war as unacceptable on the grounds that Westminster had no constitutional right to declare war on behalf of the Scottish people. The issue of the war only brought to a head deep divisions which already existed. This culminated in a battle for the leadership of the Party in 1942. William Power was the moderate, pro-war candidate supported by MacCormick. He was defeated by Douglas Young, who had come to prominence following a court case when he had refused to be conscripted. In most other respects, Young and MacCormick were allies within the Party. Young later left the SNP, after it decided membership of the SNP was incompatible with membership of any other party.

Immediately after Young's victory, MacCormick and his supporters left the Party and founded a pressure group, Scottish Convention. Within a decade, disillusionment with this approach led to calls from within for Scottish Convention to contest elections but this was not until after one of the most significant phases in the post-war history of the self-government movement. After the war and with the election of the Attlee government, it was anticipated that a Scottish parliament would be established, given the Labour Party's commitment to home rule. Scottish Convention established a series of assemblies, similar to the inter-war conventions, to discuss a scheme of devolution. The SNP, shorn of many of its moderate members, stood aloof from the assemblies, arguing that they lacked an ability to force the government to take its proceedings seriously. This was a valid criticism and the response from the assemblies was the launch of a massive petition, the Scottish Covenant, in 1948. Over two million signatures were reportedly gathered by the early 1950s, but as with the assemblies, the Covenant carried no sanction and could not force the government to act. The response of both the government and the SNP was that candidates placing home rule at the top of the political agenda required to be returned to parliament.

The failure of this phase of activity led to disillusionment and as the 1950s progressed it appeared that the home-rule movement was moribund.

Some symbolic victories were scored which acted as fillips – such as the removal of the Stone of Destiny from Westminster Abbey in 1950 and the Royal Titles court case challenging the new Queen's title as Elizabeth II on the grounds that the first Elizabeth had only been Queen of England. Though the Stone was returned to London, nationalists viewed the escapade as a victory. Four students had managed to upset the British establishment and forced the cabinet to discuss the Stone's disappearance. The decision to return it had been taken by nationalists and not because the Stone was recovered. The Royal Titles case was lost but not before a landmark judgement in Scottish legal history was made by the Lord President of the Court of Session, Scotland's premier judge, that sovereignty rested with the people of Scotland and not the Crown in Parliament (Mitchell 1996: 259–69). This was, however, the stuff of student politics, largely irreverent and insubstantial. By the late 1950s, the SNP was once more becoming the main organisation within the home-rule movement in place of the succession of pressure groups under MacCormick's leadership. Quietly and almost unnoticed the Party was building up its organisation and performing credibly, if modestly, in a few seats. In the 1955 general election it succeeded in taking second place in Perth and East Perthshire.

Leadership of the Party had passed out of the hands of the quixotic figures who dominated its earlier stage and on to a more pragmatic and disciplined figure – Robert McIntyre. McIntyre had won the SNP's first parliamentary seat in a by-election in Motherwell in 1945 during unusual wartime circumstances, only to lose it weeks later at the general election. By the early 1960s a number of those who had previously been involved in home-rule pressure groups had joined the SNP and a string of respectable by-election results kept morale high. The breakthrough came first in local elections in the mid-1960s. Suddenly, SNP councillors with limited political experience found themselves elected in a number of the large conurbations. But it was the result of the Hamilton by-election in 1967 when Winnie Ewing overturned a huge Labour majority to win the seat which brought the issue of home rule to the fore.

Ewing's defeat three years later at the general election and the Party's failure to fulfil the promise it seemed to show suggested that its support was ephemeral and based on protest votes (McLean 1970). The Western Isles was won by Donald Stewart in 1970, giving the Party its first parliamentary seat in a general election. Stewart was to devote his energies to representing his constituency and played a limited part in SNP campaigning on mainland Scotland. The rise of the SNP in the two elections in 1974 demonstrated that its support was not ephemeral and though its support collapsed in 1979 it has managed to maintain parliamentary representation continuously since 1967 and occasionally posed a serious threat to other parties. From its high point of 30.4 per cent of the vote and eleven out of seventy-one MPs in October 1974 the Party managed to hold on to only two seats and 17.3 per cent of the vote in 1979 (see Table 3.2, p. 50). The 1974–9 parliament was an exciting time in Scottish politics. At times the SNP polled spectacularly. In early 1976 it looked set to win a majority of Scottish seats but support ebbed away from the beginning of 1978 and it never recovered by the time of the election, over a year later.

The late 1970s showed up the SNP's divisions and inexperience. In parliament, its voting record often appeared confused, as over the national-isation of shipbuilding, which caused offence in the trade union movement. The Labour government's devolution proposals caused the SNP problems: should it support a measure which fell far short of the Party's objective of independence? Though divided on the matter, the SNP backed devolution and did so both in parliament and in Scotland during the referendum campaign, which culminated in a small majority voting in favour of devolution but which failed to meet the required amount set by parliament. The disillusionment which followed was an important backdrop to the bitter divisions which afflicted the Party subsequently.

The period between the referendum and election in 1979 and the next election in 1983 was the most divisive in the SNP's post-war history. An organised faction, calling itself the '79 Group, was set up within the Party supporting independence, socialism and republicanism, though little was made of the last objective by the Group. It attracted many younger Party members and much opprobrium from others. Its high point was the 1981 conference, when the Party backed a number of resolutions which the Group identified with. Most notably, the Party backed a call by Jim Sillars, a new member and former Labour MP, to support 'mass civil disobedience' against unemployment. Though having only joined the SNP the previous year, Sillars was elected a vice-chairman and joined the Party's executive committee along with other prominent '79 Group members. The '79 Group's demise came the following year after the civil disobedience policy turned into farce and Sillars and the Group were held responsible. The Party chairman, Gordon Wilson, was forced to move an emergency resolution proscribing all organised factions when a counter-group emerged in 1982, calling itself the Campaign for Nationalism, with Winnie Ewing a leading member.

The conclusion to this episode included the temporary expulsion of a number of SNP members who had been members of the '79 Group, including Alex Salmond, who later became Party leader. The SNP's poor performance in the 1983 election forced it out of this period of introspection and division. Its vote fell to 11.8 per cent and while the Party held its two seats it lost fifty-three deposits, ten more than it had lost in 1970. This sobering experience was similar to that experienced by the Labour Party in Britain at the same time. A 'new realism' emerged in both the SNP and the Labour Party. Both parties paid more attention to the electorate. In the case of the SNP, Gordon Wilson, as leader, identified three policies which he sought to change: defence, EC membership and devolution. On defence, he unsuccessfully attempted to get the Party to reverse the decision it had taken in 1981 to reject membership of the North Atlantic Treaty Organisation (NATO). The SNP had been staunchly unilateralist since the early 1960s but had wavered on membership of NATO. On Europe, he gradually moved his Party away from an anti-EC position, which had been SNP policy from the 1960s. In this he was supported by a wide spectrum within the Party, including Ewing and Sillars. Notably, he had been elected chairman in 1979 on a fairly hardline, anti-devolution platform but in time he came to believe that a *modus vivendi* had to be found between the wings of his party. He had most difficulty in getting the SNP to move away from the fundamentalist position on devolution it had adopted after 1979.

The period leading up to the 1987 election was notable more for quiet progress than any exciting breakthrough. Wilson's description of the Party as 'moderate left of centre' was accepted across the Party, allowing some to emphasise the moderate, others the left aspects of the Party's programme. The unpopularity of the Conservative government in Scotland and the growing feeling that the Conservatives had 'no mandate' to govern Scotland were important backdrops (Miller *et al.* 1981). In particular, the perception that Prime Minister Margaret Thatcher was anti-Scottish fuelled support for constitutional change.

The SNP's performance in 1987 was mixed. Both seats that it held before the election were lost to Labour but it picked up three others from the Conservatives and its vote rose slightly, to 14 per cent. But circumstances were propitious for an SNP advance. The Conservatives had lost over half their Scottish seats, Thatcher was returned as Prime Minister but was very unpopular in Scotland and Labour seemed to have won a pyrrhic victory. The 'feeble fifty', as the SNP dubbed Labour's record number of Scottish MPs, only served to draw attention to the political divide which had opened up in Britain. Legislation passed in the dying days of the 1983–7 parliament to establish a poll tax in Scotland, ahead of similar legislation for England, emphasised the point. This was the background against which the SNP fought the Govan by-election in late 1988.

The SNP had performed well in parliamentary by-elections in the past and these had played a part in boosting morale. Motherwell in 1945, Hamilton in 1967 when Ewing won and Govan in 1973 when Margo MacDonald had won were most notable but others had been important. The SNP had a formidable by-election machine, with activists pouring into the constituency from all parts of Scotland. Without having to spread its resources thinly or having to compete for attention in a British contest as occurred at general elections, by-elections had proved, even in difficult circumstances, to offer opportunities for an SNP advance. The SNP chose Sillars as its candidate and won.

The changed international context proved important for developments in the SNP. The end of the Cold War and progress in European integration aided the Party. Defence and membership of NATO were less salient. In 1988 the Party finally became firmly in favour of European integration and launched its policy of 'independence in Europe', which coincided with the launch of a push by Jacques Delors (President of the European Commission, 1985–95) for greater European integration. The SNP appeared relevant and modern. Sillars had fought the by-election on a pragmatist platform. Cooperation with other opposition parties seemed likely.

A major *volte face* occurred when the Party decided not to participate in a constitutional convention which had been launched by the Campaign for a Scottish Assembly (CSA), a pressure group established in 1980. The convention was similar to those which had met in the 1920s and the Scottish national assemblies of the late 1940s. The main difference was that Labour officially agreed to be involved. In part SNP withdrawal was due to a fear that Labour would dominate the convention, as indeed the CSA had intended to allow in order to gain Labour participation, but there was also a feeling in the SNP that the momentum achieved by the SNP would be halted through participation.

The SNP decision not to participate was the beginning of the end of the honeymoon period for the Party. The Scottish media, which had been sympathetic to the Party, turned against it. Nonetheless, there was speculation that a major breakthrough would be achieved at the 1992 general election. In the event, the SNP scored a considerable increase in its vote, gaining 21.5 per cent of the vote but holding only the three seats won in 1987, with Sillars losing Govan. The period of the 1987–92 parliament witnessed similar high expectations and subsequent disillusionment for the SNP as had the 1974–9 parliament. Wilson stood down as leader in 1990 and was replaced by Alex Salmond, who grew apart politically from Sillars, his erstwhile ally.

The situation after 1992 was, however, not as bad as after 1979. There had been an advance and good results in local elections, and the European elections in 1994 suggested that the Party still had much electoral appeal. Overall, the SNP's support fluctuated, often wildly, over the previous thirty years but a gradual upwards trend is evident. The Party is the most unpredictable and therefore threatening force in Scottish politics.

Organisation and structure

The evolution of the SNP's constitution has reflected its growth since its foundation. Considerable power is devolved to ordinary members and a highly decentralised structure exists which has made effective leadership difficult at times. Constitutional amendments require the backing of a two-thirds majority of its annual conference, making change difficult. Conference, which meets each autumn, is the main decision-making forum. Conference also elects the Party's senior officers.

Strictly speaking, the SNP has no leader but instead elects a convenor. The SNP convenor may be challenged at any conference but this has not happened since 1969 when the incumbent, Arthur Donaldson, who had held office for a decade, was successfully challenged by Billy Wolfe. Wolfe held office until 1979 when he demitted it and was replaced by Gordon Wilson, who stood down in 1989 to be replaced by Alex Salmond, the present incumbent. Other than membership of the Party, no formal qualification for office is required. The convenor need not be an MP. The style adopted by Wolfe and Wilson, though less so by Salmond, was to chair rather than lead the Party and neither man was well known in Scotland, despite serving for many years. A poll in 1981 found that only 26 per cent of SNP supporters and 13 per cent of the public at large named Wilson as one of the main leaders of the Party (*Scotsman*, 11 March 1981).

In addition to the convenor, the SNP elects a senior vice convenor (in effect deputy leader), six other vice convenors, a president, three vice presidents, a national secretary, and a national treasurer. The leader of the parliamentary group need not be and never has been the Party convenor. Donald Stewart led the parliamentary Party until he retired from parliament in 1987 and Margaret Ewing has led it since. In the late 1970s, when the Party had eleven MPs and Labour lost its overall majority in the Commons, this position was more significant than it is today. The post of president is largely honorary and is currently held by Winnie Ewing MEP. These national office bearers are joined by ten others elected by conference to form the Party's national executive committee. In part, this large body of office holders reflects the small full-time staff employed by the Party and much of the work done in other parties by headquarters' staff is done by elected office bearers in the SNP. The offices also have the merit of offering Party members something to aim for, an important consideration in a party which can offer few opportunities such as safe parliamentary constituencies to career politicians.

Between annual conferences, the Party meets in quarterly national councils, which have authority to make policy. Attendance at these meetings depends on the agenda but important decisions have been made at some meetings, most notably one in 1989 when the decision was taken not to participate in the Constitutional Convention. Though the Party has encouraged the formation of workplace branches and has a number of associations, such as trade unions, youth and student wings, the branches are the most important components in the SNP's internal structure. It is at branch and constituency level that the Party chooses candidates for public elections as well as nominations and resolutions for annual conference. Conference decisions are consequently often difficult to predict, probably more than in any other party in Scotland. Party members jealously guard against attempts by leaders to impose their will on the Party.

Electoral performance

Having the resources to contest parliamentary elections can be a major challenge for a small political party. Over the post-war period, the SNP's growing strength became evident initially in its ability to contest an increasing number of seats (Table 5.1). Its electoral successes in the 1970s were often in those areas where it had been campaigning throughout most of the post-war period. Rural Scotland and the Scottish new towns appeared more susceptible to an SNP challenge than the urban areas. However, this was largely due to the electoral system. The SNP polled well but failed to win in many Glasgow constituencies in 1974, gaining a higher share of the vote than the Party achieved in some of the seats it won that year in rural Scotland. Nonetheless, at parliamentary and local elections, the SNP has always found it difficult to make the breakthrough in urban Scotland.

The first signs of an SNP breakthrough came in local elections in the mid-1960s. In 1968 the SNP won more votes than any other party and held the balance of power in Glasgow, having received 36 per cent support. It won over 25 per cent in Edinburgh, Dundee, Paisley and Aberdeen. These

Table 5.1. The SNP's performance at British general elections

	No. of candidates	No. of seats won	% vote in contested seats	% vote in Scotland
1945	8	–	7.6	1.2
1950	3	–	7.4	0.4
1951	2	–	12.2	0.3
1955	2	–	14.5	0.5
1959	5	–	10.7	0.5
1964	15	–	10.9	2.4
1966	23	–	14.3	5.0
1970	65	1	12.2	11.4
1974 (February)	70	7	22.1	21.9
1974 (October)	71	11	30.4	30.4
1979	71	2	17.3	17.3
1983	72	2	11.7	11.7
1987	71	3	14.0	14.0
1992	72	3	21.5	21.5

From James Mitchell (1996), *Strategies for Self-Government*, Edinburgh, Polygon.

results were double edged: the Party could claim to be a serious electoral force but it would now be scrutinised as a serious political force too. The lack of maturity of SNP councillors and the differences within SNP groups soon led to trouble. This experience and the subsequent collapse in SNP support led many within the Party to argue against contesting local elections and to concentrate on parliamentary contests. SNP breakthroughs in local government in the mid to late 1970s had a similar result and again some members concluded that local government involvement was more troublesome than useful to the Party. Gordon Wilson, as MP for Dundee East, 1974–87, took this view and ensured that the Party did not contest local elections in the city for many years.

At the first district council elections in 1974, the SNP won 12.4 per cent of votes cast and sixty-two of the seats (5.6 per cent) (see Table 3.3, p. 52). At the elections in 1977 the Party was faring well in the polls during a period of unpopularity for the Labour government. The SNP then won 170 seats (15.2 per cent) with 24.2 per cent of the vote. Difficulties discussed above affected the Party's fortunes in 1980 and 1984 but a recovery was recorded in 1988 and in the last district council election the SNP won 24.3 per cent of votes cast and 150 seats (13 per cent). It also had overall control of Angus District Council and was the largest party in West Lothian. In the first regional elections, in 1974, the SNP won 12.6 per cent of the vote and only eighteen seats (4 per cent). In 1986, the SNP formed an administration in Grampian region with Labour and the Liberal Democrats. Following the 1994 regional elections they were the largest party in Tayside and formed a minority administration and continued to share power with the Liberal Democrats in Grampian. Elections to the new unitary authorities in 1995 saw the SNP win 26.2 per cent of the vote across Scotland and emerge in control of three small authorities – Angus, Moray, and Perthshire and Kinross. This was a prelude to Roseanna Cunningham's victory for the SNP in the Perth and Kinross by-election in May 1995, caused by the death of Conservative MP Sir Nicholas Fairbairn. The challenge for Cunningham and the SNP was to hold the seat at the general election, something never yet achieved by the SNP.

Policies, programmes and ideology

The SNP's constitution states its aims to be:

> a. Self-Government for Scotland – that is the restoration of Scottish National Sovereignty by the establishment of a democratic Scottish Parliament within the Commonwealth, freely elected by the Scottish people, whose authority will be limited only by such agreements as may be freely entered into by it

with other nations or states or international organisations for the purpose
of furthering international cooperation and world peace.
b. the furtherance of all Scottish interests.

Inevitably, these aims are open to different interpretations. It is, however,
notable that the Party's constitution states its objective to be 'self-government'
rather than independence, reflecting the different wings of the movement
which came together to form the Party, and though the Party campaigns
for 'independence in Europe', this has not been written into its constitution.
It is also significant that the Party does not place itself on the conventional
left–right spectrum, though throughout its history it has generally adopted
radical and left-leaning policies.

Differences exist on the issue of independence though more on how it
is to be achieved than its definition. A few hardliners in the late 1980s
were critical of the stance in favour of European integration of the Party
and argued that this negated its commitment to restoring national sovereignty
or that the EC was distant, undemocratic and bureaucratic. Significantly,
the two most vehement upholders of these views, Jim Fairlie and Isobel
Lindsay, later left the Party. Support for Scottish membership of the EU
appears to have been resolved though differences exist on the extent to
which further European integration should be supported. The support for
the European dimension is similar to earlier positions adopted by the Party.
Some within the Scottish Party set up in 1932 had supported independence
within the Empire. Later the merged party accepted that Scotland should
be part of the Commonwealth, as its constitution states. Europe, the Empire
and the Commonwealth all involved the Party finding a response to the
charge that an independent Scotland would be exposed in a hostile
international environment. As Sillars argued, a measure of economic union
with the rest of Europe would allow the SNP to argue its case for
independence without the need to combat the charge of 'separatism' (Sillars
1986: 184).

In its October 1974 general election manifesto, the SNP described itself
as 'social democratic'. This had been resisted within the Party not only by
those who did not consider themselves to be social democrats but also by
a body of opinion which viewed the adoption of any such label as
unnecessarily divisive. For the latter critics of the label, the Party ought
to concentrate its efforts on projecting itself as the supporter of independence
or self-government. Avoiding any association which might be construed as
sectional was felt to be important for a party which saw itself as 'national'.
The '79 Group attempted to give the Party a distinctly left-of-centre image.
Launched as a response to the defeats of that year, the Group was treated
with suspicion within the Party. Little was achieved in terms of policy
change by the Group – indeed, many of its members conceded that the

Party was already sufficiently left wing in policy terms – but it played a significant part in debates on the presentation of policies.

By the mid-late 1980s, the SNP had forged a fairly clear position and appeared to be at ease with the new image it had as a left-of-centre, pro-European-integration party. It had come to resemble other European regionalist and nationalist parties, the kind of parties it sat with in the European parliament. Its notion of 'sovereignty' was quite different from that which was articulated by the Conservative Party. While differences continued to exist, by the mid-1990s it had achieved a fair degree of unity around its key positions.

Relations within the national movement

The SNP grew out of the national movement but its relations with other elements of the movement have been difficult. Apart from an assortment of pressure groups, other political parties have supported home rule at times and have had nationalist-inclined factions and tendencies. The SNP's *raison d'être* was to offer an alternative to the pressure-group approach and other political parties which, even if supporters of home rule, have been viewed as opposed to home rule, unwilling to prioritise it or offering a weak measure of home rule. No formal links have been forged between the Party and other home-rule organisations though relations have not always been as difficult as in the lead up to the 1992 election.

The SNP decided not to participate in the Scottish assemblies run by Scottish Convention in the late 1940s, discussed above, but SNP members played a significant part in collecting signatures for the Scottish Covenant. The official line within the SNP on the assemblies has echoed down the years. Scottish independence would not be considered and might be attacked within the forum. The Party ought not to be too closely associated with the policy of its opponents. Some degree of cooperation was deemed desirable in the 1974–9 parliament on devolution though there was a view in the SNP that a devolved parliament might have been designed to sideline its more radical aspirations. In the event, the Party saw devolution as a first step and gave its backing both in parliament and beyond to the Labour government's measure. The failure of the scheme and the perception that it had all been a ploy to defeat the SNP took a powerful hold within the SNP in the 1980s and has affected strategic thinking since.

Relations with the CSA and the Scottish Constitutional Convention reflected this background. Though Gordon Wilson introduced a bill in parliament for an elected constitutional convention in 1980 it was to be a few years before the Party endorsed support for this strategy. The CSA convention had been designed to encourage Labour involvement but the cost was to be SNP involvement. Though the initial decision not to participate, taken in 1989, was critical of the particular scheme on offer, the line soon became that of opposition to any form of cooperation.

The 1992 election saw the defeat of Sillars as MP for Govan and his retirement from politics, though he continued to write a weekly column for the Scottish edition of the *Sun*. This strengthened Alex Salmond's position. Salmond had been critical of the manner in which the Party had decided not to participate in the Constitutional Convention and was associated with the more pragmatic wing of the Party. While Party policy did not change, its articulation did. The more pragmatic aspects of policy, largely ignored by Sillars after his election to parliament, were given prominence again. By early 1995, the pragmatic position had reasserted itself under Salmond's leadership.

The 1992 election campaign and after

The SNP entered the 1992 election in high spirits and with great expectations. Alex Neil, vice convenor in charge of publicity, had told delegates at the Party's 1991 conference that 'Scotland would be free by '93'. The poll-tax campaign had heightened the Party's profile, particularly in urban Scotland. The victory of Jim Sillars in the Govan by-election in 1988 and the defection of Dick Douglas MP from the Labour Party to the SNP a year later suggested that things were going the SNP's way. Alex Salmond found himself in the invidious position of being at the head of a party with a highly diffuse leadership with key members, most notably Sillars, setting the agenda and the pace of events against Salmond's better judgement. The SNP vote rose considerably by any normal measurement but judged against the hype and expectation of the SNP, and much of the media, it was a poor performance. The 50 per cent increase in its vote was not supported by any increase in its parliamentary representation. Indeed, both Sillars and Douglas lost their seats, the latter contesting a different seat.

The removal of Sillars from parliament, and active politics, left Salmond in an unchallenged position. His command over the Party grew, though there were a few occasions when he ran into problems. The parliamentary group voted with the Conservative government on a minor amendment to the Maastricht Treaty legislation in March 1993, provoking strong criticism from within and outside the Party.

In late 1994, the SNP reorganised its headquarters with the appointment of a new post of chief executive. Mike Russell, who had managed Salmond's leadership campaign four years before, became the new chief executive in charge of SNP headquarters in Edinburgh. The Party's financial standing had improved considerably, in part owing to a considerable bequest left by a party member. Though much media attention was paid to the Party's efforts to raise money abroad, notably in the United States, this was not the main source of its more financially secure position. To contest the next election on a more secure financial footing had been one of Salmond's main objectives following the 1992 campaign. A major fund-raising operation drew in considerable money to the Party. While this would give it a firmer base to fight the ensuing election, it would still fall far short of the resources of either the Conservative or Labour Parties.

The SNP's main problem, however, remained the strong attachment of a substantial body of voters to the Labour Party. So long as there was a fair prospect of Labour being elected to power at Westminster, the SNP would have difficulty advancing in Labour heartlands. Scottish voters are predisposed to thinking that Labour can win even without the evidence of opinion polls, by-elections and local elections in Britain as a whole. The SNP's best hope since 1992 has been to consolidate its support, target its seats wisely and prepare for a Labour government, but that has brought problems in terms of Party management, not to mention the public presentation of the SNP case.

6

The Scottish Liberal Democrats

Historical overview

While Labour may claim to be the hegemonic Scottish party in the second half of the twentieth century, the Liberal Party certainly occupied that position in the nineteenth century and for the early years of this century. Although most of that support disappeared with the downfall of the Liberal magnates, or their conversion to unionism, there are still pockets of Liberalism, which may owe their existence to the remnants of this period. They appear mostly in rural areas like the Borders, north-east Scotland, the Highlands, and the northern isles, where the working class has not been organised into Labour voting, and where Liberal crofting legislation was seen as a direct contribution to rural welfare. The radical traditions which exist in those places are still expressed through a vote for the Liberal Democrats. These concentrations of support have made Scotland important for the Party. It is not by accident that two of the Liberal Party's most important leaders – Jo Grimond and David Steel – sat for Scottish constituencies. Scottish Liberals who have played significant roles include Russell Johnston and Menzies Campbell, and recent Scottish Liberal Democrat leaders, Malcolm Bruce, and the present Scottish leader, Jim Wallace, have also been prominent in the Party at both Scottish and British levels.

The Scottish Liberal Party came into existence following the war, succeeding the former Scottish Liberal Federation. However, as in other parts of Britain, the 1960s was the decade of breakthrough for the Liberals in Scotland. While Jo Grimond had been the first Scottish Liberal to win a seat in a general election in 1950, it was not until 1964 that the Party experienced significant electoral success when the Liberals won three seats, followed by a by-election victory in Roxburgh, Selkirk and Peebles in 1965 (Johnston 1979: 82–3). The next ten years saw the advance of the SNP so that the Liberals were no longer the main challengers to the major British parties in Scotland. Although it is difficult to document this in the absence of good survey evidence, the SNP may have become the vehicle for protest votes which the Liberal Party received in England. This can be seen in Table 3.2 (p. 50), which compares Scottish and British election results since the Second World War.

The 1980s saw electoral alliance with the SDP and the official merger of the two parties in 1988, creating the Liberal Democrats. This period was traumatic. In some policies, the two groups were close; Lord Jenkins of Hillhead had expressed a sympathy with the Liberals even when he was a Labour minister. However, Liberals were not distinguished in the British political spectrum by the animus towards the Labour Party which seemed to be a most important feature of the SDP. One example of strong anti-Labour feeling among Liberals was in Greenock, where its object was Dr Dickson Mabon, the ex-Labour MP who became a Social Democrat. Much Liberal antipathy towards Labour was transferred to the Social Democrats in this case. While the alliance between the two parties was difficult to manage from 1983 onwards, the merger in 1988 was in some ways even more stressful. One difference which spanned Scotland as well as England and Wales was that the SDP was largely a party of Westminster politicians; by contrast, Liberal members put greater emphasis on community activism, and the necessity of a flexible approach towards alliances and activities, as the community situation demanded. There were though several differences affecting the relations between the parties in Scotland and England. There were few Social Democrats north of the border, and even fewer with a prominent status in the Party, with the exception of Jenkins himself, who was in Scotland only because he won Hillhead. Their low numbers led to poor organisation; where the new party was set up on an area basis containing several constituencies, many constituencies making up the area did not boast any formal Social Democratic presence. Another consideration was that some Social Democrats were not as wholeheartedly in favour of home rule as were most of the Liberals. Since this was the period when the policy became even more important for the Liberals, an additional barrier was set up between the parties. The SDP in Scotland was more conscious of Labour domination in local government, and seemed to feel that overturning this had more priority than working for a Scottish parliament. However, both parties were agreed on the necessity for proportional representation to establish more democracy, and improve their prospects, in Britain as a whole.

Organisation and structure

We have suggested that their attitudes to home rule have distinguished Liberals and Liberal Democrats among Scottish parties. We must also explore how much autonomy, in policy and other ways, the Scottish Liberal

Democrats have from the British Party. To what extent do Liberal Democrats believe that the peculiar circumstances of Scotland require freedom for the Party there to have control over its own affairs?

The Liberal Democrats are a federal party, borrowing elements of both the Liberal Party's and the SDP's organisations. The Liberal Party had a very decentralised, some would argue undisciplined, party organisation (Garner and Kelly 1993: 215). The federal structure gave considerable autonomy to the regional parties of Scotland, England and Wales, including a good deal of control over candidate selection. A separate Scottish Liberal Party was the first to be set up, in 1946 (Steed 1979: 92). Between then and 1988, there was considerable discontent in Scotland that the English Party often made statements, and was regarded in the media, as the voice of Liberalism, simply because of its greater size. Since the parties were separate, there was no Scottish representation at the English conference or on other decision-making organs. The three parties had the right to consider all matters, and not only those matters which concerned their part of Britain, and this resulted in each one preparing its own manifesto, which was sometimes at odds with the others. The Scottish Liberals, for example, had a long history of opposition to nuclear armaments, which was not always shared by the others. This chaotic situation was only possible because the Party remained so far from power and because in the event of their entering a government, policy would then be in the hands of the leader and his or her parliamentary colleagues.

The SDP, on the other hand, had a very centralised, leadership-orientated organisation. Where the Liberal Party relied heavily on the commitment of its activists (Steed 1979: 95), the SDP's main resources were its established politicians. The SDP's national committee, dominated by West-minster MPs, initiated and controlled policy (Garner and Kelly 1993: 216).

The constitution of the Liberal Democrats borrows from both component parties, bringing together some of the SDP's centralised practices with some of the pluralistic elements of Liberal Party organisation. There are three tiers of organisation in the new party: the federal, state and local levels (Fisher 1996: 95–9). The federal level includes a federal executive, federal policy committee (with two Scottish representatives out of twenty-seven) and a federal decision-making conference made up of representatives from the Scottish, Welsh and English parties. The sizes of delegations to this conference were calculated on the proportion of the Party membership contributed by each component. The state level consists of separate organisations for England, Scotland and Wales, each with their own conference. Scotland and Wales have their own executive and policy committees. England has a regional council and a coordinating committee, reflecting the regional structure within England. The local level is made up of the local parties and individual parties.

The federal conference of the Liberal Democrats is constitutionally supreme: it has complete decision-making powers over foreign affairs, defence, and macro-economic policy. The federal executive can overturn federal conference decisions and the federal policy committee, with the parliamentary party, draws up election manifestos (Fisher 1996: 97).

In practice, the federal structure of the Liberal Democrats is asymmetrical. While the state parties in Scotland and Wales retain their constitutional autonomy, the Party in England has a consultative conference only; its powers to make policy for England have been ceded to the federal conference; this also applies to some Welsh policy areas. A considerable degree of autonomy is retained at state level, including responsibility for membership. Some Scottish Liberal Democrats argue that the central (federal) party has tried to dictate beyond its competence, but to an outsider the Scottish Party seems to have a great deal of independence. It still produces its own manifesto, based on the British one. Policy in Scotland, including the manifesto, is made by a policy committee chaired by the Scottish leader.

Although the Scottish Liberal Democrats are stronger than in the past, all parties in Scotland, including the Liberal Democrats, are very under-resourced. Since the 1980s the central organisation of the Party has become more efficient, but there are several constituencies where there is no Liberal Democrat organisation. In this they have a less secure base than the other main Scottish parties. Until the early 1980s it was impossible to make a good estimate of Liberal membership since members joined their local party and there were no central records. The arrival of the Social Democrats changed this relaxed attitude and a central computerised system was installed. In 1988 there were 8,000 Liberal members and a further 2,000 Social Democrats. In 1989 this total had fallen to 5,000 after the acrimonious merger. At the end of 1994, the membership total had gone up once again to around 6,000 and remains at this level.

Electoral performance

Being largely a party of the small towns, villages, and rural areas has meant that Liberal Democrat votes count for more than if they were in towns with large electorates. The SNP has often had more votes at general elections, but has been unable to translate these into seats because its votes were thinly spread among many constituencies, including urban ones where Labour has been dominant. It is noticeable, however, that Liberal Democrats and the SNP tend to be elected in areas which are outside the main central belt and are contiguous. Liberal Democrats are particularly strong in the Highland region, and the SNP is across the border in Grampian. The Borders have a strong Liberal Democrat presence, but Nationalists are more evident in Dumfries and Galloway. The Liberal Democrats (or Liberals) and SNP seem together to have made up about 30 per cent of the Scottish vote for a long time. There have been changes in which is dominant, but a similarity has existed in the areas where they attract electors.

The electoral performance of the Scottish Liberals, Alliance and Liberal Democrats at British general elections is documented in Table 6.1. These results can be compared with the performance of the SNP, documented in Table 5.1 (p. 80).

As can be seen, support for the centre in Scotland peaked in 1983, during the period of the Alliance. In England, the Alliance won 26.4 per cent of the vote that year. An earlier indication of electoral support in Scotland had been the remarkable Hillhead by-election victory for Roy Jenkins on 25 March 1982. However, this success proved to be short lived and by 1992 support for the formally merged party had declined to nearly half that of the 1983 level in Scotland. This compared with a 19.8 per cent share of the vote for the Liberal Democrats in England in 1992.

In many respects it is more useful to examine regional variations in electoral support for the Liberals, Alliance and Liberal Democrats. Compared with the other regions of Britain, they have been relatively successful electorally in some parts of Scotland, namely the Borders and Highlands and Islands. However, there have also been some variations over time. In 1970, the Liberals were electorally strongest in Devon and Cornwall, their next two best areas being rural Wales and rural Scotland; in rural Scotland

Table 6.1. The performance of Scottish Liberal Democrats (and predecessor parties) at post-war British general elections

	No. of candidates	No. of seats won	% vote in contested seats	% vote in Scotland
1945	22	–	17.6	5.0
1950	41	2	15.7	6.6
1951	9	1	24.8	2.7
1955	5	1	31.1	1.9
1959	16	1	19.4	4.1
1964	26	4	23.4	7.6
1966	24	5	20.8	6.8
1970	27	3	14.6	5.5
1974 (February)	34	3	17.2	8.0
1974 (October)	68	3	8.6	8.3
1979	43	3	13.9	9.0
1983	71	8	24.5	24.5
1987	71	9	19.2	19.2
1992	72	9	13.1	13.1

they achieved 13.1 per cent of the vote, compared with the Scottish average of 5.5 per cent (Cook 1993: 159–60). In 1974, the Liberals improved their position in many English regions (notably the south-west) but support in rural Scotland did not increase, a reflection of the increasing influence of the SNP at the time. By the time of the 1983 election the Scottish Borders was the area of best Alliance support in Britain overall, with 54.2 per cent of the vote. They were also extremely strong in the Highlands and Islands, with 40.8 per cent (Cook 1993: 172). In 1992, although the Borders and Highlands of Scotland remained areas of strength for the Liberal Democrats, their performance in Scotland overall was poorer than in all the English regions in terms of percentage of the vote (Table 6.2).

One striking difference between developments in Scotland and England is that the English Liberals and Liberal Democrats have been much more electorally successful in local government than the Scots. In 1979, there were only thirty Liberal councillors in Scotland, compared with 800 in England. By 1994, the Scottish Liberal Democrat tally was 137, but in England there were around 4,500. It is a commonplace that one basis of Liberal Democrat strength in England has been to take up local issues and deal with them in a tactical and strategic way. Liberal Democrat councillors have been prepared to make purely local tactical alliances. In Scotland the small numbers have made this difficult, but it may be that the common support for home rule has made local arrangements unnecessary.

Following the 1992 general election, then, the Scottish Liberal Democrats had nine MPs, the Nationalists only three. With only ten English MPs, the Scottish Liberal Democrat contingent represented a more important section in the parliamentary party than previously. This has had a considerable effect on the resolution of several policies, including consolidation of

Table 6.2. Liberal Democrats' performance by region, 1992

Region	Votes	% of vote	Seats won
London	542,7333	15.1	1
South East	1,507,299	23.4	0
South West	916,905	31.4	6
East Anglia	242,886	19.5	0
East Midlands	376,603	15.3	0
West Midlands	466,048	15.0	0
Wales	217,457	12.4	1
North West	582,177	15.8	2
Yorkshire and Humberside	481,246	16.8	0
North	281,236	15.6	1
Scotland	383,856	13.1	9

From *Times Guide to the House of Commons 1992*.

the policy of home rule. Welsh Liberal Democrats also firmed up their intentions on this policy.

Ideology and policy

The philosophy of the Liberal Democrats can be seen to represent the coming together of two traditions: liberalism and social democracy. Traditional liberalism rests on the central tenet of freedom, encapsulating the themes of individualism and decentralisation, but the more modern, or social, liberal approach has advocated local and central government attempts to provide social welfare (Cyr 1988). Social democracy has tended to stress the ideal of equality, with a dual sympathy for voluntarism and statism, and incorporates an economic and social policy which involves the expansion of the welfare state, financed through a mixed economy (Bradley 1981). There are some obvious overlaps between the two traditions: rejection of class-based politics, decentralisation, internationalism, voluntarism, a belief in a mixed economy, and constitutional reform. But the merging of the two philosophies, in a very basic sense, involves an attempt to reconcile the values of individual liberty and social equality. At the time of their foundation the Liberal Democrats stated the objective of safeguarding 'a fair, free, and open society, in which we seek to balance the fundamental values of liberty, equality and community' (Pitchford and Greaves 1989: 155).

The philosophical basis of the Liberal Democrats is not contested by the Party in Scotland, and they are strongly supportive of national Liberal Democrat policies such as the mixed economy and constitutional change, including proportional representation and a bill of rights. Nevertheless, it is common for Scottish Liberal Democrats to suggest that their party is more radical than that of their English colleagues in terms of policy. It is difficult to make a final judgement on this, but there are one or two pointers. As in the case of the Labour Party, there was more support in Scotland for the antinuclear campaign, both for civil and military purposes. It is also true that although Liberal Democrats are on the whole in favour of reducing the powers of the state to interfere in the lives of its citizens, there are fewer in the Scottish Party who support the notion of economic liberalism. There is widespread support for maintaining the welfare state, as is shown in the resolutions at conference. And the Scottish Liberal Democrat conference has been known to vote for fairly controversial policy change before the English/British Party followed suit, support for the legalisation of cannabis being one case in point. Scottish Liberal Democrats are also forceful in their demands for a Scottish parliament.

Support for home rule in Scotland was the distinguishing policy of the Scottish Liberals. Sometimes, such as in the late 1950s and 1960s, this support was not an important item of their manifestos. On the other hand, this was true of Labour for a much longer time, though it is important to remember that it was the Liberal Party which formulated the idea of Irish home rule and then the extension of this to Scotland and Wales. The Party split disastrously in the 1890s over this precise policy. During the campaign to have the Scottish Covenant accepted in the late 1940s, Liberals were prominent, and one of their leaders, John Bannerman, kept this tradition alive in the early post-war years. We saw in our discussion on Liberal Party organisation that they decided to become a Scottish Liberal Party in 1946, albeit in cooperation with Liberals elsewhere in Britain. At the beginning of the current wave of support for Scottish constitutional change, Russell Johnston, Inverness MP from 1964 to 1997 when he will retire, was the first person to introduce a series of home-rule bills in the 1960s.

Despite this Party tradition, one must recall that the Liberals were never able to deliver home rule. The old Scottish Home Rule Association, made up almost exclusively of Liberal activists, had collapsed by 1906, and was refounded after the war as a predominantly Labour-based movement. In 1928, it too collapsed when the majority of its members decided that neither Liberals nor socialists could be trusted to honour their promises. From the beginning of the most recent wave of Scottish nationalism in the 1960s, Scottish Liberals have been active in support of a Scottish parliament. The pact the Liberals had with Labour helped ensure that home-rule legislation was proceeded with in parliament in the late 1970s. The Liberal Democrats have continued this tradition of support for a parliament in Scotland, taking a very active part in the Scottish Constitutional Convention. Liberal Democrats have also been important in making the case for an alternative electoral system for a Scottish parliament, and secured this in the Constitutional Convention.

Consistent support for devolution is one of the central policies, along with community politics, proportional representation, and support for Europe, which have consistently distinguished the Scottish Liberal Democrats from other parties. Nevertheless, some Liberal Democrats support the constitutional status quo. Perhaps part of this may be explained by the considerable proportion of English immigrants who are members of the Party. At the same time, one should recognise that several Liberal Democrats have shown sympathy for the idea of independence for Scotland, including Bob McCreadie, its vice president before the 1992 election.

Nevertheless, the Party's historical attachment to devolution has been very different from the SNP's advocacy of independence for Scotland. The Liberals have usually argued against devolution of responsibility for defence and foreign affairs and this crucial difference between the parties has undermined any attempts at political cooperation (Cyr 1988: 94). The importance of home rule for the Scottish Liberals and Liberal Democrats is linked with their integration into Scottish life. An important part of this is that they were able to build up good relations with major institutions in Scottish public life such as the STUC. Despite the domination of the Convention of Scottish Local Authorities (COSLA) by Labour, there has never been the bitterness between the two parties felt in some parts of southern England. The creation of the Liberal Democrats has not disrupted this relationship. Indeed, common ground has been encouraged by the proximity of Scottish Liberal Democrat and Labour policies in many fields.

The 1992 election campaign and after

Although the Liberal Democrats find themselves in a very competitive party system in Scotland, they have nevertheless had some influence in the setting of the Scottish political agenda. They were disappointed by the result of the 1992 election, and another blow to the Party in Scotland was Labour's unilateral decision to accept the idea of a referendum on home rule and on the principle of a taxing-varying power for a future Scottish parliament, contrary to the plans agreed by the Constitutional Convention. The relationship between the two parties, so close on many policies, has become more uneasy as a result.

The greatest problem facing the Liberal Democrats is that they seem unable to break into urban and central-belt Scotland. In areas where the Party is strong their MPs are well known but it is possible that the Party's reliance on these local heroes prevents it building a corporate identity. It is striking that the Party wins more seats than the SNP yet fewer votes across Scotland, and it is the SNP, not the Liberal Democrats, who are viewed with greatest fear by the Labour Party.

Part II

Scottish voting behaviour

7

Class and politics in Scotland

The fortunes of the political parties in England and Scotland are strikingly different. While the Conservatives have enjoyed electoral success in England since 1979, they have struggled to counter Labour Party domination north of the border. Now the Conservatives compete with the other parties in Scotland for the position of principal challengers to Labour.

In this chapter, we attempt to explain these developments by focusing on class politics in Scotland. Can the electoral strength of Labour and corresponding unpopularity of the Conservatives in Scotland, compared with the fortunes of the parties in England, be explained by different class distributions? Or is the explanation that similar social groups behave differently in Scotland and England? Have the skilled working class, often credited with providing Thatcher with electoral victories in England, behaved differently in Scotland?

We examine the nature of SNP support. We look at votes for the SNP in terms of its class structure. Can one say that, in some way, it is an alternative class party, although its appeal seems to be based upon national identity? There is already evidence to show that the SNP is considered a working-class party in several parts of Scotland. When we speak of a working-class party, we are referring not simply to one which attracts working-class votes, but one whose programme reflects a primary concern for working-class needs and has some success in having this accepted by working-class electors.

We also consider whether subjective class is a better indication of voting patterns than objective measures. Self-assignment to a class has been a better predictor of the vote in previous studies. We look at the level of conflict associated with class, and the relationship between class identity and national identity.

In common with the British Election Studies, we shall use the Heath–Goldthorpe classification of occupations as our measure of 'objective' class (Heath *et al.* 1991). This allows us to examine particular locations in the class structure which, according to some models, behave differently from other social groups. Where this is appropriate, we have used the convention of collapsing the salariat, routine non-manuals, and the petty bourgeoisie[1] into a category which we shall call 'middle class' whereas manual workers are called 'working class'.

Ronald Inglehart (1977, 1990) has suggested that class politics, along with other materialist orientations, are declining because people's concerns are changing and 'post-materialist' issues are displacing the hold that class politics had on the British and other electorates. As mentioned in chapter 1, environmental and other modern issues have become more salient; some have suggested that the rise of nationalism is just such a post-materialist phenomenon. We shall discuss this suggestion in more detail in a later section of this chapter.

The background

After their victory in 1979, Conservative support north of the border dwindled at successive elections. Only once since 1979 have the Conservatives reached as high as 31 per cent, their vote in 1979, in the monthly *Systems Three* opinion polls. They failed to win more than 20 per cent support in polls during 1981, though this picked up towards the end of 1982. The level for the mid to late 1980s oscillated around 20 per cent. Labour's support during the 1980s rarely fell below 40 per cent in Scotland, and was often over 50 per cent. The SNP seldom polled over 20 per cent between 1979 and 1987, but its position improved during the 1987–92 parliament. The Liberals and their successors saw their support follow the pattern of fluctuations in Britain as a whole but always at a lower level. At general elections the Conservatives did better than polls had been suggesting, Labour worse, and the SNP and Liberal Democrats about the same.

The contrast between Conservative advance in England and retreat in Scotland played a significant part in the internal politics of Labour and the SNP. The two parties began to converge as Labour emphasised home rule and the SNP emphasised its socio-economic programme. There had been talk in the early 1980s of some 'neo-nationalist' Labour MPs disrupting parliament in the event of the emergence of the 'Doomsday scenario': further victory for the Conservatives at British level while Scotland voted Labour. In fact, the 1983 election passed with no rebellions.

---

1   The five-class classification is as follows: salariat (managers, professionals and administrators); routine non-manual workers (clerks and secretaries); the petty bourgeoisie (employers and self-employed); foremen and technicians; the working class (rank-and-file manual employees in industry and agriculture).

The combination of class and nationality issues around the poll tax seemed to prove advantageous for Labour in 1987. With only 42.4 per cent of the vote, Labour won fifty Scottish seats (69 per cent) in 1987. The Conservative vote fell to 24 per cent, and the Tories won only ten seats (14 per cent). The SNP rose by 2 to 14 per cent of the vote, and won three seats (4 per cent), a net gain of one; the Alliance vote fell to 19.2 per cent, but they managed to gain an additional seat, giving a total of nine (12 per cent).

Scottish politics immediately after the 1987 election was dominated by the poll tax. This was damaging to the Conservatives, but also caused problems for Labour, as the SNP switched the emphasis of its attack away from the Conservatives, for 'imposing' the poll tax on Scotland, to Labour, for failing to use its strength to protect Scotland. Labour's historic success in gaining fifty MPs was presented as a hollow victory. This issue symbolised, perhaps more than any other, the importance of class for the SNP. The intransigence and energy of the SNP directed against the new tax marked the Party out as the key rival to Labour. From 1989, the nature of party politics returned to that of 1979. The most vitriolic exchanges were those between Labour and the SNP. Key party-political battles still centred around class and nationality, but it was within rather than across these cleavages that they took place. Labour and the SNP attempted to outbid each other as protectors of working-class and Scottish interests.

This debate formed the background to the 1992 election in Scotland. Labour and SNP competed for the vote as Scottish and working-class parties, while Tories tried to corner the British middle-class market.

Objective measures of class and voting behaviour

We begin by looking at the extent to which objective class membership explains the difference between Scottish and English voting behaviour. Do we find that there are proportionately more working-class people in Scotland in these objective terms? In other words, are the differences in British voting patterns explained away by different social class structures rather than by variations in class loyalty? We find that in Scotland the proportion of the working class, excluding foremen, fell from 59 per cent in 1981 to 49 per cent in 1991. There was a comparable, but steeper, fall in this proportion in England, from 48 per cent to 34 per cent.[2] Thus, although there remains a higher proportion of working-class people in Scotland than in England, there has been a decline in the 'natural' support base of Labour in both

---

2   Figures based on a simple manual/non-manual divide of the Registrar General's social class categorisation.

England and Scotland. Labour support in Scotland remains high despite a decline in the numbers of natural Labour supporters, traditionally a client class of unionised, manual workers.

The proportion of Labour voters among the English working class rose from 48 per cent in 1979 to 52 per cent in 1992. In Scotland, the equivalent figures were 58 per cent and 48 per cent respectively. We should remember that all classes had an option in Scotland which was not available in England, the SNP. In Scotland 27 per cent of manual workers voted for the SNP in 1992 as opposed to 16 per cent in 1979. An increasing proportion of manual workers seem to consider that the SNP is an alternative representative of their interests. Labour is not alone in representing this group.

Among the middle class, Labour is more attractive in Scotland than in England, with 30 per cent of them voting for this party in Scotland, compared with only 21 per cent in England in 1992. We must try to account for this difference. We shall examine the structural position of the Scottish middle class in an effort to do so.

The growth of the public sector and the middle-class vote

One explanation for the middle class voting Labour is that a larger proportion of these electors in Scotland, as compared with England, are employed in public-service jobs. Dunleavy and Husbands (1985) suggest that people in this sort of situation are likely to vote Labour. This may be because they have been radicalised by government cuts, threatening their own jobs and perhaps encouraged by the public-service unions, or because of an ideological commitment to maintaining government services.

There was a slight fall in public-sector jobs in England, from 32 per cent in 1979 to 27 per cent in 1992, while in Scotland the percentage rose from 25 to 30 per cent. Among middle-class public-sector workers in Scotland the proportions voting Labour increased from 28 per cent in 1979 to 33 per cent in 1992; in England there was a decline in Labour support within the same group from 35 to 24 per cent. This lends credibility to the idea that radicalisation among public-sector workers could have contributed to the increase in the Labour vote in Scotland, but we must also look at the change among middle-class workers in the private sector. In Scotland in 1979, 29 per cent of private-sector middle-class electors voted Labour, while in England only 22 per cent did so. In Scotland 35 per cent of the private-sector middle-class group voted Labour in 1992, as compared with 18 per cent in England. The proportion of private-sector middle-class Labour voters was always higher in Scotland than in England, but it went up appreciably between 1974 and 1992, whereas in England it dropped over the same period (Table 7.1). It seems consistent with these data to argue that there may have been some difference in propensity to

Table 7.1. Private- and public-sector middle-class Labour voting: differences between 1974 and 1992 survey responses

	Scotland	England
Public sector	+5	-11
Private sector	+6	-4

vote Labour between the public and private sector, but some much stronger effect seems to have operated.

The working-class vote: the influence of union membership

Trade union membership in Scotland as a whole, in line with that in Britain as a whole, declined in the 1980s. Perhaps more significant have been the areas where decline occurred. The traditional, heavy industries, once so important in Scotland, such as coal mining, shipbuilding and steel making, have declined sharply. Service industries now employ many more people in Scotland than heavy industries, and trade unions representing teachers and public employees far outstrip those representing manufacturing industries. However, this reality does not necessarily square with how the Scots see themselves. It is notable that Labour's position is stronger among trade union members than non-members: around 41 per cent compared with 30 per cent throughout the period 1974–92.

The decline in the trade union movement may have had an impact on Labour's base of support. The proportion of trade union members in manual occupations has declined from around 50 per cent in 1979 to 41 per cent in 1992. While this decline may not seem dramatic, it eats into the heart of Labour support. Among Scottish, working-class trade union members, the proportion voting Labour declined from 57 per cent in 1979 to 45 per cent in 1992. Over the same period the SNP vote rose from 14 per cent to 25 per cent.

It seems then that there are danger signals for Labour. A continuing decline in the absolute number of trade union members is potentially harmful to Labour. Secondly, the fact that the SNP made significant inroads into the working-class trade union vote at the last election is a real cause for concern for Labour. There is evidence that trade unions in general have a greater hold on the Scottish middle class than is true for England. In Scotland the percentage stands around 30 per cent, while in England the figure is 22 per cent.

Perceptions of class and voting behaviour

A number of previous studies have suggested that subjective class is a better guide to voting behaviour than objective measures of class. If class were

Table 7.2. Percentage of survey respondents identifying themselves as middle or working class, by objective categories, in Scotland, 1974–92

	1974	1979	1983	1987	1992
Salariat					
Subjectively middle class	54	39	49	54	42
Subjectively working class	39	49	48	38	55
Routine non-manual					
Subjectively middle class	24	20	21	29	23
Subjectively working class	70	73	74	67	72
Petty bourgeoisie					
Subjectively middle class	32	45	25	23	32
Subjectively working class	53	38	62	69	62
Manual foremen and supervisors					
Subjectively middle class	20	7	29	17	2
Subjectively working class	78	85	57	75	96
Working class					
Subjectively middle class	10	9	14	13	11
Subjectively working class	88	81	83	84	86

Figures may not always add up to 100 owing to rounding or exclusion of others.

of declining political importance for Britain as a whole, but not in Scotland, we should expect a decline in the percentage of those identifying with the working class in Britain, whereas this should not have happened in Scotland. In fact, the percentage identifying as working class in Scotland rose from 68 per cent in 1974 to 74 per cent in 1992. In England, for the same period, there was a decline of those identifying as working class, from 65 to 57 per cent. This suggests that there have been different trends in class consciousness in the two countries.

Table 7.2 shows that since the mid-1970s Scottish voters have maintained their identification with, or increasingly identified with, the working class, despite objectively being classified as one of the higher social status categories. But how have these trends affected voting patterns?

We might hypothesise that voting Labour would be strongly associated with working-class identification. We can see from Table 7.3 that this is so, but interestingly there have not been large changes. Support for Labour remained pretty constant among the working-class identifiers. In England the situation was that 46 per cent of those identifying with the working class in 1979 voted Labour; in 1992 the equivalent figure was 49 per cent.

Table 7.3. Subjective class and vote in Scotland, 1974–92 (%)

	1974	1979	1983	1987	1992
Middle class					
Did not vote	9	8	20	14	13
Conservative	39	60	33	39	41
Labour	17	12	13	14	15
Liberal	10	10	26	21	14
SNP	24	9	6	9	15
Number of respondents	310	152	82	95	214
Working class					
Did not vote	12	12	18	16	15
Conservative	14	21	13	16	16
Labour	40	42	43	41	37
Liberal	6	7	15	17	8
SNP	25	16	9	9	22
Number of respondents	802	458	265	211	703

Since we know that the percentage identifying as working class has gone up in Scotland, the contrast between the two countries is again consistent with the importance of the SNP's working-class appeal, which has no equivalent in England. The SNP have made a fairly large impression on working-class identifiers in Scotland.

This is confirmed by comparing party supporters' subjective class in Scotland and England (Table 7.4). The results reflect the greater intensity of working-class feelings in Scotland overall: all party supporters feel more 'working class' than their English counterparts. However, we also see some interesting differences between the parties. The Conservatives, in Scotland and England, are relatively evenly split between working- and middle-class consciousness. Labour supporters in Scotland are almost entirely working class in perception, followed by the SNP, particularly since 1983. The subjective identities of SNP supporters are unquestionably similar to those of Labour supporters.

We should note the changes in class identity of smaller groups in the class structure; the most interesting cases are the salariat and, secondly, the foremen/women and (manual) supervisors. In 1992 over half the Scottish salariat perceived that they were working class, compared with 39 per cent in 1974. This may be associated with changes in the working conditions and prospects of this group: the so-called proletarianisation of the middle classes. There has also been a suggestion that, with increasing affluence, manual supervisors would be more likely to consider themselves part of

Table 7.4. Party supporters by subjective class: Scotland (England) (%)

	1974	1979	1983	1987	1992
Conservative					
Working class	43 (45)	44 (47)	51 (45)	43 (49)	54 (43)
Middle class	48 (49)	41 (46)	40 (46)	52 (46)	41 (49)
Other	9 (6)	15 (7)	9 (9)	5 (5)	5 (8)
Labour					
Working class	84 (78)	78 (77)	89 (76)	83 (78)	87 (78)
Middle class	13 (18)	7 (18)	9 (19)	13 (19)	11 (19)
Other	3 (4)	15 (5)	2 (5)	4 (3)	2 (3)
Liberal/Alliance/Liberal Democrat					
Working class	56 (57)	58 (58)	73 (53)	62 (59)	65 (49)
Middle class	38 (37)	28 (37)	24 (39)	31 (34)	33 (44)
Other	6 (6)	14 (5)	3 (8)	7 (6)	2 (7)
SNP					
Working class	70	72	82	66	80
Middle class	26	13	15	34	17
Other	4	15	3	0	3
Total number of respondents	1175 (1588)	623 (1596)	402 (3341)	352 (3275)	797 (2064)

management, and thus identify with the middle class, where before they might have felt more solidarity with other manual workers. Our results provide evidence consistent with this in the earlier period after a Labour government, but virtually all of these electors identified with the working class in 1992.

The conclusion from the above is that Labour is regarded as a class party in Scotland and both the middle class and the working class give their votes to it on the basis of objective or self-perceived class on a larger scale than is true in England. Also, the SNP is seen as a working-class party now more than it was in the past.

It may be that the Scots have a more conflictual model of class than the English. Sartori (1976) distinguishes between 'cleavages of identity' and 'cleavages of conflict', suggesting that some cleavages simply make those on one side or the other aware of their position while other cleavages bring them into active opposition. Although we find that there was an increase in class identity, most notably an increase in working-class identity, as well as an increase in perceived levels of conflict, there is little evidence to suggest that Scottish voters have a more conflictual view of class politics than English voters. In answer to a question asking them whether there was bound to be conflict between the classes, 54 per cent in both countries agreed with this proposition. There was no difference between the working-class and middle-class electors in England and Scotland. The perception in both countries and for both classes led to the same level of Labour voting.

The challenge of a new identity

It is becoming clear from this discussion that it would be a mistake to consider class identity in isolation. Although class identity is important for voting behaviour in Scotland, and is now recognised as such by both Labour and the SNP, this does not necessarily imply that the passage between the two parties is based on class identity. It is possible that national identity (to be examined in greater detail in chapter 10) has assumed a greater importance and it is this which may tempt voters to move from Labour to the SNP. The relationship between the vote and national identity is displayed in Table 7.5.

As we have argued elsewhere (Brand *et al.* 1993), the level of both class and national identity was higher in 1992 than in 1979. In 1979, 84 per cent of the sample acknowledged having a class identity and 91 per cent acknowledged a national identity; by 1992 this had risen to 96 per cent and 98 per cent respectively. How do the two identities compare? A much higher percentage of Scottish middle-class electors gave priority to their national identity than to their class identity. When asked whether they had more in common with an English person of the same class or a Scottish person of a different class, 25 per cent chose the fellow member of the middle class, and 46 per cent chose the fellow Scot. Among working-class respondents, the equivalent percentages were 32 and 44. Despite the dominance of the class party, social proximity seems to reside in a similar

Table 7.5. National identity and vote, 1992 (%)

	Scottish not British	Scottish more than British	Equally Scottish and British	British more than Scottish
Did not vote	16	16	13	10
Conservative	10	14	34	53
Labour	30	36	30	17
Liberal Democrat	4	11	10	12
SNP	38	22	11	5
Other	2	2	2	2
Total number of respondents	184	384	314	58

ethnic identity. This may be a reason why Labour, a working-class party, has taken national claims so seriously. It might also mean that the SNP has a greater potential for growth. It seems that the combination of class and national identities creates a distinctive form of politics in Scotland.

Class politics or post-materialism?

The importance of the national community can be based on several sorts of concern. It may be that those who are concerned with the nation want to promote its economic health; for them the national economy is more important than the economic health of any class within it. Some writers, however, believe that nationalism is about cultural values rather than economic ones. Nationalists may be prepared to sacrifice prosperity for the goal of national self-government. This latter point leads us to consider the importance of post-material values, since some scholars suggest that nationalism is linked to the pre-eminence of post-material over material values.

Inglehart argues that European politics were about the basic conditions of life up to about the 1960s (Inglehart 1977, 1990). After that time, many citizens no longer needed to worry about material shortages and basic security. They were able to devote themselves to other (post-materialist) demands such as freedom of speech and the right to participate in decisions about their own future. Politics would more and more concern itself with these sorts of questions, but the older generation in each system would still place most emphasis on material security, disadvantaged members would share this approach, and there might be countries and regions where the old priorities persisted. In general, however, modernisation would involve a change to post-bourgeois values; with this change might come new parties or radically new programmes for the old parties.

We have tested some of the propositions which are implied by this model. Mostly we used the items in Inglehart's post-bourgeois scale,[3] but there are other relevant questions in the Scottish and British election surveys; for example, we asked about support for environmental protection, the use of nuclear energy for peaceful or military purposes, and greater equality for women. With these indicators, we look at support for 'post-bourgeois' positions, the differences between generations, between England and Scotland, and between the classes.

The need for maintaining order in the nation, one of the materialist items, is given the first priority by a very large margin, both in Scotland

---

3 Respondents were asked to choose the two most important goals from the following: maintaining order in the nation; giving people more to say in important government decisions; fighting rising prices; protecting freedom of speech.

and England. The second most important item, again in both countries, was the other materialist choice, fighting rising prices. Consistent with this, the post-materialist items are chosen by very few of the respondents in both countries. The overall picture does not show much evidence of an interest in these issues.

If the post-materialist model is appropriate, class differences in politics ought to decline in the face of the new issues for electors who are economically and in other ways secure. Middle-class citizens ought to show more concern for post-materialist issues. Nearly 50 per cent of non-manual workers choose 'maintaining order in the nation' first, as compared with 33 per cent of manual workers, and there is a slightly lower percentage of non-manual workers who are concerned with freedom of speech. Otherwise there is no significant class difference in the rest of the distributions, and the differences which we have noted are in a direction opposite to what the model would suggest.

While we are discussing basic demographic divisions, it is worth noting here that there is no evidence of generational differences. It is not true in either country that younger people are less materialist. We have some questions other than Inglehart's which touch on the question of post-bourgeois values. Of all these, younger people are more opposed to the development of nuclear power, but they are not different on any other issue.

Conclusion

Class is still an extremely relevant feature of voting in Scotland. Our work has simply indicated that the nature of this relationship is different from its English equivalent. It is clear that, among those who would be classified objectively as 'middle-class', a higher proportion vote Labour in Scotland than in England. This is quite separate from middle-class Scottish voters who vote for the SNP, whether they agree with its 'class party' attitudes or not. Scotland and England also differ in the extent to which those who are objectively middle class are prepared to identify themselves as working class, and from this to vote for Labour or, in smaller numbers, the SNP. To conclude, class, subjective more than objective, is still a good predictor of the vote in Scotland but the voter's decision is influenced by the existence of other identities. There are other, distinctly Scottish, dynamics at work which complicate class models of voting in the Scottish context.

8

Religion and politics in Scotland

In his study of west European politics, Yves Mény identified three major elements in the relationship between religion and politics: the relations of churches to the state; the relations of churches to society; the relations of religious values to political values (Mény 1991: 22). Relations of the churches to the state range from 'total separation to quasi-identification between a dominant Church and the State apparatus' (Mény 1991: 22). Church–society relations may involve churches limiting themselves to a 'strictly religious role, avoiding any competition with the State; sometimes, on the other hand, they establish an outright counter-society, reacting against the interventions of a State whose legitimacy or policies they challenge' (Mény 1991: 25). Church values may to a greater or lesser degree influence, correspond with or be contrary to those of society.

These three relations will form the basis of our analysis of religion and politics in Scotland. However, before discussing each of these key relationships in turn, it is important to note a number of dangers inherent in the study of religion and politics. It is easier to identify the existence of social identities, including religious identity, than it is to understand their political meaning and significance. As we have previously noted, individuals will often have a range of different identities. An identity may have significance in a particular context and then be of little or no significance in another context for any individual. The catalyst or context which gives rise to an identity becoming politically salient is therefore important.

Scots are predominantly Protestant, with just over half our respondents in 1992 identifying themselves as such, but a substantial minority (16 per cent) identified themselves as Catholic. These figures are similar to those obtained in 1979. The proportion of Catholic identifiers in Scotland is higher than in England. In both countries, those brought up as Catholic are far more likely to retain that identity in later life than are Protestants. Similarly, a higher proportion of Catholics are regular church attenders.

It is important to be wary of parochial and pathological assumptions, that is, assuming that something which exists or occurs in one place is peculiar to that place or somehow strange or 'unnatural'. Much of the debate on religious identity in Scotland, at least at a non-academic level, appears intent on demonstrating that Scotland is different or even perverse. By ignoring what occurs elsewhere or choosing to draw limited comparisons (for instance, comparisons only with Ireland) or by concentrating only on the less attractive aspects of the relationship between religion and politics, a very limited and indeed inaccurate picture will emerge.

It is also important to recognise that the elements listed above in the relationship between religion and politics are inter-related. The legacy of church–state relations may be evident in the relationship between church and society and that between religious values and political values.

Relations between church and state

The historical context is important in understanding the relations between church and state. The 'pure' form of a dominant church was a feature of politics in the nineteenth and early twentieth century, most notably in Italy, but also to some extent in England. A much more fluid situation prevails today. Being an established church has less significance in the late twentieth century than it had in the nineteenth century.

It has been argued that the Church of Scotland 'cannot be regarded as "established" in entirely the same way as the Church of England' (Bochel and Denver 1970: 68). This was maintained because it was the product of a fairly recent union (in 1929) of established and disestablished factions. However, the changing role of the Church of England, leading it to become a forum in which sharp criticisms of the government and the 'established' political party – the Conservative Party – are voiced, has arguably led to a marked change in the relationship between the state and the Church of England. Similar changes have occurred in Scotland during the same period, which largely coincided with the premiership of Margaret Thatcher.

Being an established church may offer certain privileges but this does not prevent decline. Indeed, it has been suggested that perhaps the 'worst thing for religion in England' was the establishment of the Church of England (Greeley 1992: 68). This appears also to be the case in Scotland. Having the status of 'establishment' does not appear to provide protection from secular trends.

Until the late nineteenth century the Kirk in Scotland had considerable influence in terms of administrative arrangements. Local administrative arrangements were based on the parochial organisation of the Kirk and developed in the era of 'ad hocery'; through the reforms of local government in the twentieth century, most notably from the 1929 Reorganisation Act, they moved towards larger units organised increasingly around the principle of *ad omnia* authorities, though there was inevitably a legacy in terms of local boundaries. The reorganisation of local government in the 1970s and again in the 1990s ended any links with church arrangements. The development of the welfare state, the wider range of local authority services provided, the need for larger units of local government and the development of multifunctional authorities were part of the process of secularising the administrative arrangements evident in the twentieth century.

The most notable service affected by the Church of Scotland, as indeed has been true elsewhere, was education. Ad hoc committees for administering education at the local level in Scotland in the period 1872–1929 were based on the organisation of the Kirk and these provided the main religious–political battleground in Scottish politics. The Scotch Education Department had to intervene in disputes. Significantly, Catholics in Scotland saw this bureaucratic form of administration and government as offering safeguards to their community: 'it was a relief to the Catholic, who had feared that a completely Scottish department might have proved bigoted' (Skinner 1967: 26). It is also worth noting that among those MPs who attempted to reform the law before 1918 to provide support for Catholic schools in Scotland were Irish MPs (Skinner 1967: 26). One of the legacies of this period was the perceived need, as late as the 1960s, to provide 'unusually strict' requirements for protecting teachers from arbitrary dismissal (Skinner 1967: 71).

The 1918 Education (Scotland) Act is best known as the legislation which brought Catholic schools under the state sector. It also reformed the central administration of education, consolidated and rationalised central educational grants and officially changed the name of the Scotch Education Department to the Scottish Education Department. The Catholic community was largely a poor immigrant community and the prospect of its members advancing were limited. The main issue of controversy in the original bill had been the proposal to abandon the ad hoc basis for the local organisation of education. The issue of bringing the Catholic schools into the state sector was relatively uncontroversial; indeed, the only obstacle appeared to be the possibility that Catholics themselves might refuse to accept the settlement. The Act's provisions were, therefore, a form of 'positive discrimination', that is, intended to tackle an existing imbalance. State education at that time was effectively Presbyterian. School boards were replaced by education authorities administering whole counties and burghs. As a means of offering an immigrant community a stake in society, acknowledging and accepting religious pluralism and minimising grievances and potential conflict, it is difficult to view the Act as anything other than a success. However, the legacy of the Act is disputed. The secularisation of state education is sometimes seen as having weakened the case for separate schools but any

Table 8.1. Attitude to Roman Catholic schools in Scotland and religion (%)

	No religion	*Catholic*	*Protestant*	*Other*
Separate schools	12	52	15	21
Phase out	88	48	85	79
Number of respondents	229	145	455	91

attempt to assess its impact must take account of the possibility that without it the Catholic community might have been less integrated, less capable of advancing and inter-communal tensions considerably greater.

In terms of church–state relations there has been a marked change over the course of the twentieth century. The Kirk remains established but this has had little political significance. The most lasting legacy has been in the field of education. The 1918 educational settlement still stands. Catholic schools still exist and have been controversial. These controversies have been concerned with whether the state should provide funding for Catholic education and, more recently, with falling school rolls, whether local authorities can afford to keep these, and other state schools, open. Our survey conducted in 1992 suggests that there is widespread support (79 per cent) for phasing out separate Catholic schools (Table 8.1). However, care must be taken with these findings as 'phasing out' can be interpreted as a (very) long-term objective. Even among Catholic identifiers, around half support phasing out separate schools, although this includes lapsed Catholics. Among Catholic regular church attenders (those who attend Catholic religious services once a week or more), however, there is majority support (66 per cent) for the retention of separate schools.

The high proportions of Catholics favouring the phasing out of separate schools may well be explained by the timescale perceived by those supporting 'phasing out' the schools. Additionally, this may well represent the sense of 'belonging' to Scottish society more generally and a weakening of the sense of being under threat which was a feature of the Catholic community in early decades.

Relations between church and society

A number of political scientists have noted the importance of religious cleavages in politics. Foremost among the works considering social cleavages is Lipset and Rokkan's work (1967), as discussed in chapter 1. Traditionally religion has been important in European politics. The politics of Christian democracy were not the only evidence of the impact of churches on political parties. Within the communist and socialist parties there was an anti-clerical tradition but there was also within the socialist parties a Christian socialist tradition. In European countries such as Italy, France and Germany, fairly tight networks of institutions created by and related to the churches exist. Anti-clerical political reactions have historically been common. The consequence of the proliferation of institutions was the 'tendency to consider every question in clerical or anti-clerical terms and to by-pass class distinctions in the name of common membership of the same religion' (Mény 1991: 27). Education was the most notable area in which this was evident. Emmanuel Mounier's *personaliste* philosophy was influential among French socialists. The most notable French socialist politician to have been influenced by *personalisme*, which stressed non-Marxist, anti-individualist principles, in recent times has been Jacques Delors, whose speeches throughout his political career have been sprinkled with references to Mounier. On the other hand, others have identified the emergence of 'new politics', focusing on new cleavages such as environmental protection, women's liberation and greater democratisation of society, which replace old cleavages such as class and religion (Dalton 1988: 134).

In Scotland, the relationship between Catholicism and the Labour Party and unionism (rather than Conservatism) and the Unionist/Conservative Party looks less unusual when set in the European tradition. In large measure this development resulted from immigration. Indeed, it might be more accurate to draw a parallel with American politics, where waves of immigrants played an important part in developing the social cleavages affecting that country's politics. Irish immigration, particularly in the 1920s, a time of economic decline, was blamed in much the same way as immigration elsewhere at other times (in Germany today for example) for the difficulties. Catholic support for a party of the left – which might seem a curious phenomenon in other European countries where Catholicism is associated with support for parties of the right – is explained by the fact that this is the support given by what was often a poor immigrant community to the party seen as most likely to be sympathetic to the least well off. In that sense, Labour's historic strength among Irish Catholics resembles the support given to the American Democrats by Irish immigrants.

One of the consequences was the effect this had on Labour Party politics. Frank Bealey's classic 'peasant's stockpot' analogy of the ideology of the Labour Party (Bealey 1970: Introduction) – with the different elements added at various stages with certain elements flavouring the mix to a greater or lesser extent at different times – would have to include Catholicism in Scotland. There has been little discernible evidence of an anti-clerical tradition in Scottish politics, within the Labour Party or any other. This may go some way towards explaining why Labour in Scotland was less inclined to follow the sub-Marxist Bennite route in the 1980s. More importantly, the Labour Party's links with Catholicism played a significant part in integrating the Catholic immigrant community into Scottish society.

Of course, there was a reaction against this which was articulated through the Unionist Party. Changing its name to 'Unionist' from 'Conservative' in 1912, the Party deliberately set out to tap into latent anti-immigrant, anti-Catholic sentiment in Scotland. In the 1920s, prominent Conservatives were publicly active members of the Orange Order and vehemently anti-immigrant speeches were made. The consequent polarisation of politics was eventually weakened by the class cleavage. Class cut across religion but initially appears to have affected the Protestant working class. The Unionist share of the Unionist/Conservative vote has declined over the post-war period without any compensating increase in its share of the Catholic vote. Labour, on the other hand, was much more successful in holding on to its working-class and middle-class Catholic vote. It is difficult to determine whether this process was brought about by structural changes in Scottish society or whether the Party itself facilitated its own decline by changing its name back to Conservative from Unionist in 1965. The behaviour of the Party has certainly changed. The Conservatives today, and for many years, have been determinedly opposed to sectarianism. Now, there is little evidence of Conservative working-class Protestant support.

The difficulty for third/fourth parties was that the cleavages – both class and religion – were relatively dichotomous and rigid. The voting system probably accentuated this dichotomy. Evidence from 1974 and 1979 showed the difficulty which third/fourth parties had. It proved easier to make inroads into the Protestant vote for the Liberals and SNP – as the Labour Party had done. It was more difficult to win Catholic support. As Miller explained:

> A new party, rapidly gaining support and with a generally popular policy, might be best able to turn sympathy for policy into voting support among the least integrated, most atomized, least organized, sections of society. Supporters of an old party going through a phase of unpopularity would be more likely to stay loyal to it if they had a high level of social contact with other supporters. It would be more difficult for a new party to win flash support from a socially and politically integrated group than from a collection of individuals. (Miller 1981: 146)

Despite the fact that Catholics had fairly typical views on constitutional reform they were only a third to a half as likely to vote SNP as other Scots in 1974 and the irreligious were pro-SNP without being specially pro-devolution (Miller 1981: 173).

As late as 1979 this situation prevailed. By 1992, as Table 8.2 demonstrates, the Scottish Catholic community remained loyal to Labour though less so than previously. Labour has historically played an important part

Table 8.2. Percentage voting for different parties by religion, 1992 (1979)

	No religion	Catholic	Protestant	Other
Did not vote	20 (17)	18 (13)	11 (10)	16 (10)
Conservative	15 (22)	6 (10)	30 (39)	24 (42)
Labour	31 (38)	53 (67)	27 (24)	27 (36)
Liberal Democrat	9 (7)	7 (2)	9 (10)	12 (7)
SNP	23 (15)	16 (7)	20 (15)	18 (–)
Other	1 (2)	– (1)	3 (3)	4 (7)
Number of respondents	235 (218)	148 (88)	477 (392)	97 (31)

in the integration of the Irish Catholic community into Scottish society. Ironically, this success may itself be the reason for the evidence that Catholics are beginning to move away from the Party. As the Catholic community feels increasingly self-confident and identifies with Scottish society, the extent to which religious affiliation plays an important part in voting behaviour may well decrease. This is not the same process as secularisation which appears to have affected the Protestant community.

Labour remains the party most favoured by Catholics and there remains strong Catholic hostility towards the Conservatives. Conservatives do best among Protestants though this is likely to be a function of the antipathy felt towards the Party by Catholics and the irreligious. Significantly, the SNP has gained support among the Catholic community. On balance, most Catholics look on the SNP quite favourably. This does not mean that they will vote for the Party but it is an important first step. Given that it was among this section of Scottish society more than any other that the SNP had greatest problems attracting support in the 1970s, this will be welcome news to the Nationalists.

In a comparison of religion in Britain, Ireland and the United States, Greeley notes the difference between the development of Methodism in England and the United States. In the former, social respectability was sought by Methodist leaders, while in the latter, Methodist leaders appealed to immigrants pouring into the east and the pioneers moving west:

> So religion perhaps provided a community function that it did not in Britain (save perhaps for the Irish immigrants). Religion also became an essential part of the social location and self-definition of Americans. (Greeley 1992: 54)

It has not only been Methodism which has been afflicted in this way in England. In Scotland Presbyterianism provided an important 'community

Table 8.3. Long-term policy for Northern Ireland and religion (%)

	No religion	*Catholic*	*Protestant*	*Other*
Remain part of Britain	30	21	51	53
Reunify with rest of Ireland	62	76	45	42
Other	2	1	1	1
Northern Ireland as independent state	1	1	–	1
Up to Irish to decide	6	2	4	3
Number of respondents	205	127	405	79

function' but this has lessened. As Greeley notes, the 'community function' of Catholicism for Irish Catholics in Britain, including Scotland, has been very important. The 'community function' in the case of Scottish Catholics has been related to the maintenance of identification with Ireland and the protection of the rights of immigrants.

An additional consideration will be the relationship between the religious community and its political views. Religious groups may function in a number of ways, most notably in sharing the beliefs and doctrines of the church. They may also be a social group in a wider sense. A substantial number of Scottish Catholics are second- or third-generation Irish immigrants and, consequently, have distinct views on Irish politics. The survey data (Table 8.3) show very strong support (76 per cent) among this group for the reunification of Ireland as a long-term policy. Significantly, a substantial proportion of Protestants (45 per cent) also favour this policy. This suggests that the unionism of the Protestant community has waned considerably while the Catholic community has maintained much of its attachment to Ireland. Notably, substantial numbers of irreligious people (62 per cent) support reunification as a long-term policy.

In terms of the relations of churches to society, Scotland has witnessed a complex phenomenon. A range of social institutions have existed and exist which help maintain the link between the churches and society, most notably the Catholic Church. Among the political parties, the dichotomy of Catholic–Labour versus Protestant–Unionist (Conservative) is now less sharp than it once was. The rise of the SNP may have played a part in this but it is as likely that the SNP has been a beneficiary of this process rather than its cause. As might be expected, the community which has retained its link with a particular party has been the Catholic link with Labour. Even that may be beginning to change. Once more, the evidence suggests that the Catholic community feels more secure as a part of Scottish society. Protestantism appears to have lost much of its earlier political meaning among those who identify with it. Though Seawright and Curtice are correct to argue that there are a number of reasons for the decline in Conservative voting, their conclusion that the decline 'cannot be accounted for by an erosion of the religious alignment in Scotland' (Seawright and Curtice 1995: 339) is tendentious. While it is true that the proportion of Conservative voters who are Protestant has not declined, this is only a small part of the picture. Many Protestants who in previous times would have been expected to vote Conservative no longer do so. The Conservatives have been palpably unsuccessful in maintaining the grip they once had on the Scottish Protestant working class. The Conservatives remain a Protestant party, though far less successful in this respect than previously. More significantly, the sharp Protestant–Catholic dichotomy has been damaged. Especially since 1992, knowing an elector's religion cannot be used so confidently in predicting party preference.

Relations between religious values and political values

It is difficult to measure the extent to which religious values influence political values. The decline of church attendance need not result in the link between religious values and political values being broken. Many of the values we take for granted probably originate in the teachings of the various Christian churches. Mény speculated on this point:

> We may well wonder whether, despite the declining impact of Church institutions and personal Christian allegiances, Christian values have not become such an integral part of certain societies that they persist quite independently of the religious services and practices that expressed them in the past. (Mény 1991: 29)

In this respect, we might expect that there is little difference among the different Christian denominations on a range of issues. It is indeed difficult to identify social issues on which there is a clear difference between the denominations. However, we might expect clearer support or opposition among a particular denomination for some issue. One such issue is abortion. The Catholic Church is emphatically opposed to abortion. Catholics remain much more opposed to abortion than Protestants and those denying a religious identity, but a significant shift has taken place since 1979 within the Catholic community. Whereas 46 per cent of Catholic identifiers felt that the availability of abortion on the National Health Service had gone much too far in 1979, only 16 per cent thought this in 1992. While only 22 per cent felt that abortion's availability was about right in 1979, 41 per cent thought so in 1992.

Once more, care must be taken in interpreting the data. The context has changed. Abortion was arguably less salient as a political issue in 1992.

Table 8.4. National identity and religion, 1992 (%)

	No religion	Catholic	Protestant	Other
Scottish not British	23	26	16	14
Scottish more than British	45	37	39	39
Equally Scottish and British	28	30	36	35
British more than Scottish	2	1	4	5
British not Scottish	2	1	4	4
None of these	–	5	1	1
Other	–	–	1	1
Number of respondents	235	148	477	97

Additionally, as has already been noted, Catholic identifiers will include people with a cultural rather than devout attachment to the Church and will not necessarily accept its doctrines and beliefs. The large proportion of Catholic identifiers who think that the availability of abortion on the National Health Service is 'about right' may well only be indicating the limited extent to which abortion was a salient issue. It is quite probable that in the event of a bill coming before parliament or some other means by which the issue rises on to the political agenda then a different set of views would emerge. It is also worth noting that among regular church attenders a very different pattern prevails: 67 per cent of Catholics who attend services regularly believe that 'abortion has gone too far'.

The relationship between religious and national identities is complex. In the past, Scottish identity was often associated with Scottish Protestantism. Opposition to Irish Catholic immigration earlier this century was often articulated in these terms. Catholicism came to be associated in political discourse with anti-Scottishness in some sections of Scottish society. Catholics might have been expected to oppose Scottish home rule, fearing that this would mean Protestant rule. But equally, the Irish nationalist links of many

Table 8.5. The constitutional issue and religion (%)

	No religion	Catholic	Protestant	Other
Independence from Britain and EC	6	6	6	5
Independence from Britain within EC	24	23	14	14
In Britain, with assembly	48	52	51	54
No change	21	19	28	27
Other	1	–	2	–
Number of respondents	230	142	468	94

of the Catholic community has meant that British identity has been unappealing to many Catholics in Scotland. Indeed, Britishness has often been associated, through the issue of Northern Ireland's constitutional status, with Protestantism. We might expect to find Catholics in Scotland reluctant to adopt a British or Scottish identity and perhaps instead opt for an Irish identity. Among Catholics in Scotland, 70 per cent identified themselves as Scottish, 20 per cent as British and only 5 per cent as Irish. Among Catholics in England, a tenth identified themselves as Irish.

Notably, Catholics are more likely to identify themselves as Scottish than are Protestants though the difference is not great (see Table 8.4). The fact that most people in Scotland see themselves as predominantly Scottish should be noted. Whether this has political (and constitutional) implications may be another matter (see Table 8.5). In fact, Catholics are more likely to support constitutional change than are Protestants. A sizeable minority of Protestants retain a unionist position on the constitution – but it should be stressed that this is a minority.

Conclusion

In the first section of this chapter the focus was on the relations between churches and the state. Here it was seen that the relationship between politics and religion has changed dramatically over the course of the twentieth century. Earlier emphasis on the position of the Kirk gave way to the position of state over the issue of support for separate schools. It would appear that the church–state relations have lost much of their significance. Even among Catholics there is a trend towards support for secular education.

In the second section, we considered the relationship between the churches and society. Clearly, this is not a comprehensive account of church–society relations, which would have to include the great variety of organisations and networks established by the churches and those through which they operate. But even excluding these, it is clear that church–society relations are far more extensive and meaningful in contemporary Scotland than church–state relations. Change has, however, occurred. Most notably, the links between the denominations and the political parties have lessened and this was more so the case at the 1992 election than at any previous election. It is doubtful whether the Conservative Party can re-engage support in the Protestant community. It would be difficult to do so and potentially electorally damaging. There can be no certainty that it would succeed but every likelihood that sections of existing Conservative support might move on. A different problem confronts Labour: how to regain its almost hegemonic position with the Catholic community. In order to hold on to this support,

Labour will have to recognise that old appeals to Irish identity may be useful but are unlikely to be sufficient any longer.

In the third section of the chapter, we discussed the relationship between religious values and political values. Again, this is difficult to measure. There is evidence that this aspect of the relationship between religion and politics continues to have significance but has weakened in recent years. Religious denominations do not correspond as clearly with attitudes on abortion as they once did. Similarly, religion is less of a guide to understanding voting behaviour than it used to be. Catholics today overwhelmingly see themselves as Scottish. Indeed, a higher proportion of Catholics support the SNP policy of independence in Europe than do Protestants.

The main conclusion of this chapter is that in Scotland, as elsewhere in western Europe, religion is less significant politically than it once was. The Catholic community in Scotland now feels confident and secure in its Scottish identity. In recent years, senior members of the Catholic hierarchy have suggested that the Scottish Catholic community has 'come of age'. The evidence of this chapter confirms this suggestion.

9

A nation of rational voters?

Following changes in society since the 1960s and the perception that class voting went into decline it is now common to view the decision to vote as a rational act. Many analysts have documented the decline in aligned voting and the apparent rise of 'judgemental' or 'issue' voting (Rose and McAllister 1986; Crewe 1992; Denver 1994). While there is debate about the exact nature of change involved there can be no doubt that voters are now less loyal, and that major issues can and have disturbed previous voting patterns.

A number of attempts to explain recent voting patterns have used a variant of the 'economic voting' hypothesis (Denver and Hands 1992; Sanders 1993). Such theories suggest that the decision to vote is in some way related to the state of the economy, but economic voting may have many manifestations. In this chapter we attempt to assess the utility of such approaches in understanding the decision to vote in the 1992 general election in Scotland. The Scottish Election Study provides us with micro-level data which can be used to analyse the influence of respondents' subjective views of economic conditions on their voting choice. Such an approach cannot measure the influence of objective economic conditions on actual political behaviour (macro-level analysis). At the time of the 1992 election, objective economic indicators suggested that Scotland's economy was in fact outperforming that of the rest of Britain for the first time since 1974 (Seawright and Curtice 1995: 338; Bell and Dow 1995: 45). However, what is important in the discussion of voting behaviour is the effect of voters' perceptions of economic developments.

If economic conditions affect behaviour there are a number of ways in which this may occur. We begin by outlining some models of economic voting which may be relevant in the Scottish context. All theories of economic voting are based on the assumption that voters attribute responsibility to government for the state of the economy. If voters do not in any way hold government responsible for the economy, locally or at the level of the state as a whole, there is no basis for understanding voting using economic theory. While economic prosperity or discomfort may exist this can take on electoral significance only if people make a link between the activity of government and economic performance.

The most common approach is the reward–punishment hypothesis, otherwise referred to as pocketbook voting. This is a retrospective approach which predicts that voters reward or punish the government for economic conditions. It assumes the economy is a 'valence' issue rather a 'position' issue. Butler and Stokes distinguished between 'position issues, on which the parties may appeal to rival bodies of opinion, and valence issues, on which there is essentially one body of opinion on values or goals' (Butler and Stokes 1974: 292).

Group-based theories assume that parties will pursue policies which are broadly consistent with their core, class-related, group of support. In this case the economy is seen as a position issue; it is assumed that decision makers can choose different sets of economic outcomes which will benefit different groups of voters. Thus, an economic strategy based on high rates of unemployment would not benefit lower occupational groups. These approaches may be based on short-term or long-term expectations. Sociotropic approaches reject the individualistic, or egocentric, assumptions of many economic voting theories. Instead, the individual voter is said to be affected by the well-being of the community of which he or she is a part.

While the relevance of many of these hypotheses has been tested at the British level (Heath *et al.* 1991, 1994) our interest lies in the attitudes of Scottish respondents and how, if in any way, they differ from those of English respondents. In an effort to understand different voting patterns in Scotland we consider a number of questions which arise from the various economic theories of voting. How do Scots perceive the state of the economy? Are their perceptions of the economy more or less optimistic than those of English respondents? To what extent do the Scots attribute responsibility for economic performance to the government? Is it correct to regard the economy as a valence issue in Scotland? What are respondents' personal economic experiences and how important are they in their choice of party? Is there any evidence of pocketbook voting in Scotland? Do Scottish respondents regard area- or national-level economic prosperity as more important than individual economic affluence?

Perceptions of the national economy

Measuring perceptions of the state of the economy is a difficult exercise as 'the economy' has many different elements. For this reason, SES respondents were offered a wide range of questions relating to the economy. To begin with, respondents were asked to give their opinion on the state of Britain's economy in 'the last year' and in the 'last ten years'.

Table 9.1. Perceptions of Britain's economy (%)

| | Economy in last year | | Economy in last 10 years | |
	Scots	English	Scots	English
Got stronger	10	12	27	32
Got weaker	53	53	19	19
Stayed same	33	30	47	41

On the whole, very few differences emerge between Scottish and English respondents on the performance of the British economy. Both sets of respondents were very critical of economic performance in the year before the 1992 general election, but only one in five of all respondents felt the British economy had weakened in the previous ten years (Table 9.1). The Scottish respondents were a little less likely to have perceived a strengthening of Britain's economy over the longer period. However, we should not overemphasise the differences between the Scottish and English respondents on the question of national economic performance. They are definitely more similar than dissimilar.

Personal economic experience

Our next objective was to assess how respondents perceived their personal level of economic wealth, as opposed to the general strength of the British economy. Respondents were asked a number of questions about their individual economic prosperity. In answer to the question of whether household income had kept up with prices, there is no difference whatsoever in the Scottish and English responses: 47 per cent of all respondents claim that their household income has fallen behind prices and 12 per cent have experienced a rise compared with prices. And when it comes to 'their own standard of living', fewer Scots claim to have experienced a fall in their standard of living, although the differences are not substantial (26 per cent of Scots, 29 per cent of English).

So far there appears to be little support for the suggestion that Scottish voters feel worse off than their English counterparts. However, some interesting differences begin to emerge when we introduce a comparative element to the questions. When asked to compare their household incomes with those of other British families, Scottish respondents are less inclined to indicate that their income has risen more than average: 20 per cent of English respondents indicated such a rise, against only 15 per cent of the Scots. Around a third of all respondents claimed to have experienced a fall in household income compared with other British families. Scottish voters begin to appear more distinctive when asked the reasons behind

Table 9.2. Area compared with other parts of Britain (%)

	Scotland	England
Much more prosperous	3	7
Little more prosperous	12	17
Stayed above average	30	32
Little less prosperous	29	24
Much less prosperous	23	15
Level of prosperity a result of government policy	68	53

changes. Importantly, 51 per cent put this down to government policy whereas only 43 per cent of the English regard such changes to be the direct result of government policy.

Economic prosperity of area

So far, the attitudes of Scottish and English respondents have not differed greatly. The biggest differences arise when respondents are asked to compare the prosperity of their area with other parts of Britain. While nearly one in four English respondents regard their own area as more prosperous than other parts of Britain, only 15 per cent of the Scots felt this way about the prosperity of their area (Table 9.2). Over half the Scottish respondents, 52 per cent, regarded their area as less prosperous than other areas in Britain. And when it comes to responsibility for differences in the area's prosperity, it is quite clear that respondents in Scotland are much more likely to blame government policy.

Attribution of responsibility

Even though Scottish respondents are not particularly more negative about the state of the economy or about their own economic position, there are some signs that, when compared with other respondents, they do feel less prosperous. Most significantly, Scottish respondents are considerably more likely to place responsibility for economic problems at the door of the government.

The tendency of the Scottish respondents to see government as responsible for managing the economy is reflected in attitudes towards a number of issues involving government activity. Scots are a good deal more likely to view government as responsible for providing jobs and a good standard of living for all, and they are more likely to want government to make a greater effort to equalise incomes and to get people back to work rather than keeping prices down. The majority of Scots claim that redistribution issues influence the way they vote: 54 per cent agree that 'efforts to equalise incomes' are an important influence on the way they vote (a minority of the English respondents agreed with this statement). Thus, the Scots as a nation appear more interventionist. The Scottish respondents express a preference for a high level of government involvement in the economy in order to ensure a fair distribution of wealth. Management of the economy involves a number of choices and the Scots clearly reject the free-market approach to economics, and to a greater extent than the English. Therefore, it could be argued that the economy is not a clear-cut valence issue in Scotland. It could be that attitudes towards government intervention indicate the expression of an ideological position.

Thus, the distinction between the economy as a position issue and a valence issue is not altogether clear. Even if we accept that a prosperous economy, however managed, is seen as 'good for all by all', in other words the economy is essentially a valence issue, we might argue that in the Scottish case there are other valence issues which challenge the economy as an explanation for voting patterns. For instance, on a whole range of social welfare issues the Scottish respondents want more from government and less from the market: 60 per cent of Scottish respondents agree that 'income and wealth should be redistributed', compared with only 45 per cent of the English respondents; and 27 per cent of Scots, against 16 per cent of the English, think the government 'should get rid of private education'.

These findings lead us to suggest that the Scots have different issue priorities (Mitchell and Bennie 1996). To a greater extent than the English, they want their government to take responsibility for education, health[1] and the reduction of poverty. It is government performance in a very wide sense that concerns the Scottish respondents. Theories of pocketbook voting appear limited in their attempts to explain what matters to Scottish voters. At the very least, as has been argued by Heath *et al.* (1991: 147), these theories should be widened to include a more general assessment of government performance.

A closer look at personal economic experience

Egocentric approaches to economic voting assume that voters act to maximise their own economic prosperity. If voters do behave 'egocentricly' we would expect to find that people who had achieved a relatively secure economic position would have different attitudes and party preferences to those people who had experienced relative economic misfortune. In an effort to test this

1   While 60 per cent of Scottish respondents think National Health Service standards have fallen since the 1987 election, 49 per cent of English respondents agree.

Table 9.3. Profile of respondents with rising living standards since 1987 (%)

	Scotland	England
Should encourage private medicine	29	36
Should get rid of private education	23	12
Government should spend more to create jobs (strongly agree)	26	19
Voted Conservative in 1992	33	54
Conservatives are a caring party	49	61
Labour are caring	71	69
Liberal Democrats are caring	72	79

hypothesis we begin by comparing the attitudes of the third of respondents in Scotland and England who claimed to have experienced a 'rise in their standard of living since the 1987 election'.

This look at the better-off individuals in Scotland and England mirrors the overall differences in Scottish and English responses. The Scottish 'better-offs' are rather more sceptical about the private market and are more in favour of government action on the whole (Table 9.3). However, the biggest differences appear in attitudes towards the Conservative Party. While the majority of English respondents with rising living standards view the Conservatives favourably, and indeed voted for the Party in 1992, the same cannot be said for their Scottish counterparts, only a third of whom voted Conservative in 1992, and 40 per cent of whom consider the Party 'uncaring'. By contrast, both groups agree on the caring qualities of Labour and the Liberal Democrats. Thus, it would appear that individual economic prosperity in Scotland is less strongly correlated with support for the Conservative government than in England.

Another way of assessing the importance of individual prosperity is to compare the differences between the economically advantaged and dis-advantaged, whom we term 'risers' and 'fallers', in England and Scotland, and see if this is linked in any way with opinion on issues, attitudes to parties, voting and turnout. In Scotland is there more or less of a difference in attitudes between the economic risers and fallers? We begin by looking at respondents who indicated an improvement in their household economic experience over the last ten years and responses of those with falling living standards, bearing in mind that Scots as a whole do not claim to be worse off. If the differences between these two groups are smaller in Scotland, we might conclude that personal economic gain is not as likely to affect the outlook of respondents. In other words, if Scottish respondents are more homogeneous we can tentatively conclude that attitudes do not appear to be influenced by economic prosperity.

Table 9.4. Beliefs in areas of government responsibility (%), by rising/falling prosperity over the last ten years

	Scotland	England
Strongly agree that government should spend more to create jobs		
Risen	23	20
Same	33	21
Fallen	47	36
Government should spend more to get rid of poverty		
Risen	52	49
Same	58	49
Fallen	73	63
Government should put more money into National Health Service		
Risen	57	55
Same	68	62
Fallen	84	70
Government should spend more on education		
Risen	60	63
Same	61	50
Fallen	73	67

When we compare attitudes on the role of government (Table 9.4), in both Scotland and England we find that those with falling incomes are more 'interventionist' but in Scotland there is an even bigger discrepancy between 'risers' and 'fallers'; those with falling incomes are even more interventionist.

Thus, perhaps contrary to expectation, the Scottish respondents are actually less homogeneous – they are more polarised. While those who are better off in both countries look very similar, those who feel worse off in Scotland form a relatively distinct group; management of the economy appears to be a position issue for these people. This is illustrated by their tendency to blame government directly for their fall in economic fortunes. Of those who experienced a fall in household income in the last ten years, 64 per cent of English and 70 per cent of Scots blame government, thus satisfying the first condition of economic voting. We might expect that this group is likely to punish the government. It is certainly the case that on all matters of government intervention – tax cuts, equalisation of income and so on – the Scots with falling incomes were most likely to say these issues influenced their vote.

In England, economic 'risers' are predominantly Conservative, and in Scotland being a riser certainly increases one's chances of voting Conservative

**Table 9.5. Personal economic experience over the last ten years
and the vote (%)**

| | Conservative | | Labour | | Liberal Democrat | | SNP |
	Scotland	England	Scotland	England	Scotland	England	Scotland
Risen	27	54	23	17	11	16	19
Same	27	46	28	25	9	14	22
Fallen	13	26	43	42	9	17	18

but overall the votes of the better off are really quite evenly distributed across the parties (Table 9.5). However, economic 'fallers' are clearly pro-Labour in both countries; almost exactly the same percentage of fallers vote Labour in both samples. Interestingly, the SNP receive a similar level of support from all types of voters, whether they have experienced a change in economic prosperity or not. The pattern which emerges is that economic fallers in England and Scotland are strongly inclined to vote Labour, but only the better off in England are clearly pro-Conservative. Therefore, there is no strong link between economic prosperity and voting Conservative in Scotland. We conclude that experiencing economic prosperity in Scotland does not greatly increase the chances of voting Conservative. Indeed, one in three of those people who fared well over the ten years describe themselves as 'anti-Conservative', and 43 per cent consider the Conservatives 'uncaring' (cf. 21 per cent and 32 per cent in England).

These conclusions are further illustrated by examining the effects of 'popular capitalism' in Scotland. It has been shown elsewhere that the sale of council houses and shares in privatised companies had a positive effect on the Conservative vote in Britain (Garrett 1994). However, the evidence at the Scottish level is much less convincing. The total number of respondents who might be termed popular capitalists is much lower in Scotland than in England. Fewer Scottish respondents purchased privatised shares; fewer have private health insurance; they are less likely to own two cars; and they are less likely to own their own property or have a mortgage.

Even those Scottish respondents who might qualify for the term 'popular capitalist' are much less likely to vote Conservative than in England. While receiving services from the private market greatly increases chances of voting Conservative in England, the strength of the relationship is much weaker in Scotland. This would explain why the government's 'right to buy' scheme failed to bolster the Conservative vote in Scotland. Although many Scottish people did take advantage of the scheme, the purchase of a council house in Scotland does not increase the chances of an individual voting Conservative to any significant extent (cf. Brand *et al.* 1994: 217).

To sum up our findings so far, Scots do not feel worse off at the individual level, but those who do feel worse off seem to form a distinct group in Scotland; they are more interventionist than those who have gained over the last ten years. Overall, the responses are more polarised in Scotland. However, this does not translate directly into polarised voting patterns. While economic losers do appear to vote for the party most likely to represent their interests and against the party of government during the period of their economic decline, those who have gained economically do not appear substantially more likely to vote for the party in government during the period of their economic improvement. Therefore, something else must be at work to explain why those individuals who have become more prosperous do not seem inclined to reward the Conservatives.

A closer look at prosperity of the nation/area

One possible explanation is that the state of the national (British) economy is more important to voters in Scotland than personal wealth. If this were the case we would expect to find a discrepancy in attitudes regarding individual prosperity and perceptions of the economy. In actual fact we find it is almost impossible to separate these. Our study suggests that there is a very strong relationship between individual experience and perceptions of the British economy's prosperity. We find that over 80 per cent of all respondents who felt better off in the last ten years also indicated that the British economy had either strengthened or stayed the same. Only 18 per cent of the Scottish 'better-offs' and 13 per cent of the English 'better-offs' felt that the British economy had weakened. Conversely, those respondents who are worse off at the individual level are rather disparaging about the state of the national economy: in both countries only 20 per cent of those who feel worse feel that the economy has improved. Thus, the Scottish and English give very similar responses when asked about the British economy. However, it is a quite different matter when we ask about the prosperity of the respondent's own area (Table 9.6).

We find that few of the Scottish respondents, whether better off or worse off personally, feel that the prosperity of their part of Britain has increased. Less than one in four of those Scots who feel better off think the same about their area, and nearly half indicate that their area has become less prosperous over the years. The contrast with the English respondents is clear: nearly 40 per cent of the English who feel better off think their part of Britain has also prospered, while less than a third detect a fall in prosperity. In sum, the better off in Scotland are also likely to see the British economy as healthy but their perceptions of the part of Britain in which they live are very different indeed. These findings lead us to consider

Table 9.6. Prosperity of individual and area in last ten years, Scotland and England (%)

	Area more prosperous	Same	Less prosperous
Scotland			
Respondent better off	24	27	49
Respondent worse off	9	25	66
England			
Respondent better off	37	31	32
Respondent worse off	15	32	53

whether the explanation for different voting patterns in Scotland is to be found in perceptions of area prosperity.

It is certainly the case that Scottish respondents are more likely to detect a worsening in the prosperity of their area, but, even more significantly, they are also much more likely to blame government policy directly for this: 87 per cent of Scots, compared with 68 per cent of English. In addition, those Scots who feel that their area has suffered are clearly more in favour of government spending to remedy the situation. This perhaps explains why those Scots who perceive a drop in their area's prosperity are so anti-Conservative. Only 12 per cent claim to have voted Conservative in 1992 and 65 per cent describe the Party as 'uncaring'.[2]

National identity is given close examination in chapter 10, but in the context of this discussion we find that it is closely related to perceptions of area decline. While we should be cautious about the causal direction of the relationship, 75 per cent of those Scottish respondents who detect economic decline in their area consider themselves more Scottish than British, compared with 46 per cent of those who perceive an economic improvement in their area, and 60 per cent of the entire Scottish sample. Those Scots who consider their area to be in decline are also the most likely to see the advantages of independence for Scotland: 39 per cent think independence would make Scotland better off (23 per cent of 'area more prosperous'). Unsurprisingly, this group are the most likely to have voted SNP in 1992. However, this same group do not argue that independence would make them personally better off: only 16 per cent indicated such an expectation. This finding reinforces the view that the Scottish responses are more sociotropic than individualistic.

2   In England, 31 per cent of respondents claiming to come from a less prosperous area voted Conservative in 1992 and 53 per cent consider the Conservatives uncaring.

Conclusion

In assessing economic expectations in Scotland we have found that Scots are no more pessimistic about the strength of the British economy than respondents in England. Nor do the Scots indicate lower levels of personal economic prosperity. However, those Scots who have experienced improvements in personal wealth during a period of Conservative government differ markedly from their English counterparts in the way they vote. Personal economic gain in Scotland does not tend to result in rewarding the (Conservative) party of government.

What appears to be important to Scottish voters is the prosperity of their area, relative to other areas in Britain. There is evidence to suggest that Scottish respondents perceive a decline in the prosperity of their area over the last decade or so and, more importantly, they attribute responsibility for this to the policies of the Conservatives. Scottish respondents reject the Conservative free-market approach to economic management and in this respect the economy resembles a position issue in Scotland. However, it is government performance in a very general sense that concerns the Scottish respondents.

In discussing the uniqueness of Scottish voting patterns we must consider perceptions of Scotland's relationship with England. It is surely no coincidence that nearly half of all Scottish respondents think that England's economy benefits most from having Scotland in Britain. Only 14 per cent think that Scotland's economy benefits more from being part of Britain. And it is the Conservative Party that suffers most from this perception. It is clear that voting in Scotland is complicated by national identity and the Scotland–England relationship. We examine the dynamics of national identity in the following chapter.

10

National identity in Scotland

National identity is notoriously difficult to measure. An individual's national identity, and that of the wider community, may change over time. The strength of national feeling and its political significance are not constant. They are affected by context. The same person may identify strongly with Scotland when the national football team is playing England's but side with Britain during a general election and even more so with Britain during a period of international tension or war.

National identity is a collective identity. It involves having a collective memory, shared experience and, most notably when discussing contemporary politics, a view of a collective future. Anderson has described nationalism as the formation of an 'imagined community' (1991). By this he meant that people collectively associate with each other even though they may not know each other; 'in the minds of each lives the image of their community' (Anderson 1991: 15). In this sense the community is 'imagined', and though it is created in the mind it may be no less real and important than a community of people known to each other. The collective memories which help create a community and the myths and stories which inform these memories are important.

Nationalism may also refer to a political programme. Gellner has argued that nationalism is 'primarily a political principle, which holds that the political and national unit should be congruent' (Gellner 1983: 1). The distinction between nationalism as a form of collective identity and nationalism as a political programme is important. As a collective identity, a Scot may feel culturally Scottish but this need have no political or constitutional implications. As a political programme, Scottish nationalism demands the establishment of some measure of self-government. In the case of Scotland, there are at least two national identities, Scottish and British, though it should be noted that these identities need not be in competition but may be complementary.

National identity is only one identity an individual will have and one identity may undermine or strengthen another. Among these identities are gender, space or territory, class, religion and ethnicity. Another important identity is party identity. Identification with political parties has been in decline but remains important (Crewe and Denver 1985; Schmitt and Holmberg 1995). What may cause one identity to become politically salient for one person may not have the same effect for someone else. As Rokkan and Urwin note, identities are benign or antagonistic depending in each instance upon the 'particular concatenation of events, policies and trends' (1983: 114). Religious identity is one other identity held by individuals. Kamenka has argued that religion and nationalism are a 'frightening mixture indeed, though in religion as in nationalism, one has to be backward-looking to be really terrifying' (1993: 91). Religion may have played a part in forging the Scottish nation, as other nations, but this may have little contemporary political significance.

The relationship between ethnicity and national identity can be equally frightening. Those who are not deemed ethnically 'pure' are often denied rights as nationals or citizens. However, the civic notion of the nation is a predominantly spatial or territorial conception (Smith 1991: 9). Belonging to the nation does not presuppose membership of a religious, ethnic or other social group but will be open to all those living within the community. As Smith has noted (1991: 13), every nationalism contains civic and territorial elements in varying degrees and different forms.

The nature of Scottish national identity

Subjective feelings of national identity are difficult to study in any context. Nationalism in Scotland is no less difficult to measure or explain. In fact, the existence of a dual national identity in Scotland makes the analysis of national identity even more complex. Scottish people may feel part of the Scottish community while also feeling loyal to the British state and nation. Cultural and political events will influence feelings of national identity at different times. So, we can expect that feelings of national identity in Scotland are likely to fluctuate over time.

Nevertheless, there is some evidence that in recent years attachment to the Scottish national identity has intensified. Election Study findings indicate that at the time of the 1992 general election, Scottish national identity was particularly strong in Scotland. Following the election, respondents were asked the question 'Do you consider yourself to be British, Scottish, English, Irish or something else?' Nearly three in four Scottish respondents (72 per cent) chose the 'Scottish' option and only one-quarter the British option. Only 1 per cent chose Irish. In 1979 only 51 per cent of SES respondents described themselves as Scottish and over one-third, 35 per cent, considered themselves British.

The Scottish identity also appears strong when we compare it with identities in the other regions of Britain. In 1992, only 31 per cent of respondents living in England chose to describe themselves as English, 63 per cent as British. Of Welsh respondents, 55 per cent considered themselves Welsh and 34 per cent British. However, there is a problem in understanding English national identity as this is probably not distinguished from British national identity in the same way as is Scottish national identity. In England, the terms 'England' and 'English' are often used as synonyms for 'Britain' and 'British'. So although the bare figures suggest that English national identity is weaker than Scottish national identity, this is not necessarily the case.

Clearly, a Scottish national identity exists. Scottish people do feel part of a Scottish community; they collectively associate with each other. However, does this Scottish identity compete with the British identity, or are these identities complementary? Do Scots feel Scottish and British? Through the SES we are able to examine the apparently competing Scottish and British identities. Table 10.1 displays responses to a question asking about the relative importance of the two identities.

On the one hand, these results can be seen to support the notion that the British and Scottish identities are complementary: in 1992 three-quarters of Scots saw themselves as both Scottish and British. On the other hand, we should not underestimate the strength of the Scottish identity. One in five Scots reject the British label outright and nearly three in five at the very least see themselves as more Scottish than British. We should also note that these responses were gathered at the time of a British general election, when electors are focused on British issues, and this is likely to suppress nationalistic feelings. Opinion poll findings have also suggested that people in Scotland have a more 'Scottish' than 'British' identity but these are less scientifically conducted and not in the context of an election campaign.

Table 10.1. Scottish and British identity in Scotland, 1992 (%)

	Percentage of sample
Scottish not British	19
More Scottish than British	40
Equally Scottish and British	33
More British than Scottish	3
British not Scottish	3
None of these/not applicable	2
Number of respondents	957

Perhaps more important than an awareness of national identity is perception of conflict between nationalities. Scots might be quite prepared to describe themselves as Scottish rather than British, but is this based on a real conflict between the Scots and the English? In other words, is the cleavage of identity translated into a cleavage of conflict? Again, the surveys provide some evidence that this is indeed the case. SES respondents were asked in 1979 and 1992 if they believed that conflict existed between the two nationalities. The numbers identifying conflict between the Scots and the English increased substantially, from 58 per cent in 1979 to 81 per cent in 1992. Also, in 1992 over 40 per cent of Scottish respondents were of the opinion that 'people in Scotland generally disliked people in England', although only 14 per cent were willing to admit that they themselves disliked English people. Therefore, it would appear that perceptions of conflict have become more intense in recent years.

So much for illustrating that a national identity cleavage exists. It is perhaps more important, certainly more difficult, to identify what people living in Scotland mean when they say that they feel Scottish, British or a combination of these. One possible source of national identity is a country's cultural heritage: literary, linguistic or historic traditions that inspire national pride in contemporary society. However, McCrone has argued that nationalism in Scotland is not built on strong cultural traditions (1992: 214). In an effort to understand the importance of Scotland's cultural heritage Scottish respondents in 1992 were asked to identify from a list of eight items what made them most proud of Scotland.[1] They were also asked about those things which made them most proud of Britain. A very small number of the Scottish respondents, only 10 per cent, said that they were most proud of Scotland's history, and only 2 per cent chose Scottish art, music or literature. The two most popular choices were 'the people' (35 per cent) and 'the countryside and scenery' (30 per cent). Therefore, our findings support those of McCrone. Attachment to Scottish cultural heritage does not appear to be a major determinant of Scottish national identity. The Scots are most proud of those things which make up modern Scotland – the people living there and the countryside and scenery surrounding them. This becomes even more apparent when we compare these with those things which make Scottish people proud of Britain. While 'the people' was still one of the most popular choices, this amounted to just one-fifth (21 per cent) of the responses, and only 14 per cent claimed to be most proud of the British countryside and scenery.

---

1   The eight items on the list were: the countryside and scenery; the people; history; sporting achievements; art, music and literature; education and science; legal system; democratic tradition.

Table 10.2. Percentages of nationality identifiers and other identities

Other identity (% of sample)	Scottish identifiers	British identifiers
Gender		
Female (53)	50	58
Male (47)	50	42
Age		
18–34 (32)	36	26
35–54 (35)	36	34
Over 54 (33)	28	40
Religion		
Roman Catholic (15)	19	13
Church of Scotland/England (50)	46	56
No religion (25)	28	20
Class (Heath–Goldthorpe)		
Salariat (20)	17	25
Working class (41)	47	32

By contrast, many respondents (21 per cent) identified the democratic tradition of Britain as a source of pride. Only 6 per cent referred to Scotland's democratic tradition. It seems that British national identity rests more heavily on political tradition than Scottish identity.

As we noted earlier, national identity is but one of many identities. Several other identities are intertwined with feelings of nationality. These include gender, generation, religion and class identity. The Election Study data allowed us to begin to assess how these identities relate to national identity, if at all. We compared all those respondents who felt more Scottish than British (the two categories of 'Scottish not British' and 'more Scottish than British' in Table 10.1) with those respondents who at the very least felt equally Scottish and British (the three categories of 'equally Scottish and British', 'more British than Scottish' and 'British not Scottish'). Thus, we divided our sample into two groups by creating one group of Scottish identifiers, 'Scots', and one group who displayed a British identity at least as strong as their Scottish identity, therefore labelled 'Brits'. The Scottish identifiers represent the largest group (Scots, 60 per cent; Brits, 40 per cent).

So what is the relationship between national feeling and the other types of identity? Some of these relationships are explored in Table 10.2. To begin with gender, on the face of it males appear to have a stronger Scottish identity, although the difference is not substantial. A wider discrepancy emerges between age cohorts. Respondents with a strong Scottish identity are much more likely to come from the younger cohorts than those with a British identity. Indeed, British identifiers are considerably older than the sample as a whole: 40 per cent of this group is 55 or over. Scottish identifiers are less likely to be religious, but they are more likely to be Catholic. British identifiers are quite solidly Protestant. This should not surprise us. Many Catholics are of Irish origin or identify with Ireland and may be loath to associate with Britishness given the connotations that has in debates on Ireland. Therefore, their 'Scottishness' may be as much a function of their opposition to Britishness as a positive affirmation of Scottish national identity.

Class and the economy

The relationship between class and national identity is complex. When we compare Scottish identifiers and British identifiers it becomes clear that 'British' respondents are objectively more middle class. Based on the Heath–Goldthorpe occupation classification (Heath *et al.* 1991), 'British' identifiers are more professional. All objective indicators support this conclusion. Respondents with a British identity are more likely to have attended a private school than Scottish identifiers; they have more qualifications; they are a little less likely to be members of a trade union; they are likely to own their own home but are unlikely to have bought it from a local authority. In all these respects the differences between British and Scottish identifiers are not substantial but they all go in the same direction, leading to the conclusion that, objectively, British identifiers are more middle class.

Subjective indicators (self-classification of respondents) support these findings. Respondents with a strong Scottish identity are much more likely to perceive themselves as working class. 'Scots' are also more likely to perceive conflict between the classes. While 59 per cent of Scottish identifiers believe that 'there is bound to be conflict between classes', only 48 per cent of British identifiers agree that this is the case. These results point to the existence of two relatively strong cleavages – class and national identity. However, evidence of the greater intensity of national identity is provided by the claim of 45 per cent of the entire sample that they have more in common with Scots of the opposite class than English people of the same class. Only 26 per cent of all respondents felt that they had more in common with English people of the same class. Even those respondents with a British identity indicated that they had more in common with Scottish nationals (39 per cent) than people of the same class in England (29 per cent).

Respondents with a strong Scottish identity are more critical of the performance of the economy and are less optimistic about its prospects: 34 per cent of British identifiers are of the opinion that the British economy got stronger in the last ten years compared with only 22 per cent of Scottish identifiers. Furthermore, a larger share of Scottish identifiers believe they are falling behind in terms of standard of living: 51 per cent of Scots (41 per cent of Brits) believe their household income has fallen behind prices. Scots are also more likely to think that their area is less prosperous than other parts of Britain: 28 per cent of Scots think their area is much less prosperous, compared with only 18 per cent of British identifiers. Significantly, Scots are also more likely to blame government policy directly for this. As for opinions on future economic performance, British identifiers are definitely more optimistic about the British and Scottish economies. While 30 per cent of British identifiers think the Scottish economy is likely to 'get stronger' in the next year, only 16 per cent of the 'Scots' agree, and 44 per cent of the British, against 29 per cent of the Scots, think the British economy will get stronger.

One of the largest differences to emerge in the responses of Scottish and British identifiers is in their view of how much Scotland and England benefit from being part of the union. Respondents with a Scottish identity are much more likely to indicate that England enjoys more benefits: 60 per cent of Scots think England benefits more, only 31 per cent of Brits. British identifiers are most inclined to believe that the relationship is about equal. Therefore, the Scottish identity appears in some way to be related to economic pessimism and the perception that England receives more benefits from the union. On a whole range of economic issues Scottish identifiers are rather negative in outlook. They are more likely to think that since the last election prices have increased, taxes have increased, and unemployment has increased.

The perception of Scotland's relationship with England is clearly an important aspect of national identity. It is difficult to measure the extent to which anti-English feeling exists in Scotland as we have to suspect that direct questions asking whether respondents are anti-English probably do not elicit honest answers. A very small number of our respondents (14 per cent) claimed to 'dislike the English', the vast majority indicating they neither liked nor disliked them; however, just over one-quarter of Scottish identifiers revealed their personal dislike for the English. We also asked what our respondents thought was the attitude of Scots in general, rather than themselves in particular, regarding the English. A very significant number of respondents in each identity category (over 40 per cent) believed that the Scots disliked the English. Those people who see themselves as exclusively Scottish or British are most inclined to believe that conflict exists between the Scots and the English. Those respondents who consider themselves 'Scottish not British' are the most likely to agree that the Scots dislike the English a lot, followed by those who see themselves as 'British not Scottish'.[2]

National identity and political issues

Consistently, Scottish identifiers are more likely to support government intervention in the economy (Table 10.3). They are more likely to agree that it is the government's responsibility to provide jobs and a good standard of living and less likely to agree that welfare benefits have gone too far. They are more likely to oppose privatisation and support trade unions. These attitudes are consistent with the class backgrounds of Scottish and British identifiers.

Both EU membership and defence have been issues which have been debated by the parties in Scotland in a distinct way. The launch of the SNP's 'independence in Europe' campaign in 1988 and the support for unilateral nuclear disarmament in the SNP and the Scottish Labour Party until its 1996 conference suggest that Scottish opinion might differ from British opinion. In fact, there was little discernible difference between British and Scottish identifiers as far as EU membership is concerned. Scottish identifiers are a little more likely to favour increasing the powers of the EU but also a little more likely to agree with the proposition that membership involves giving up traditions. Scottish identifiers believe that the government should spend less on defence and are less in favour of having nuclear weapons. They are also much more critical of building nuclear power stations: 60 per cent agree building has gone too far, compared with 40 per cent of British identifiers. In essence, Scottish identifiers tend to be more left wing.

Parties, constitutional change and national identity

During the late 1980s, the Conservatives were accused by their political opponents of being anti-Scottish and, as we mentioned in chapter 4, an enquiry by two Scottish Conservative vice presidents following the 1987 election concluded that the Party had fared badly because it was seen as 'English and anti-Scottish' (Mitchell 1990). This would lead us to expect that people with a strong Scottish identity would be most likely to view

---

2   The question asked: 'How much would you say that people in Scotland liked or disliked people in England? Would you say that they liked them a lot, liked them a little, disliked them a lot, disliked them a little, or does it depend on the person?' Twenty-two per cent of 'Scottish not British' and 15 per cent of 'British not Scottish' agree that 'Scots dislike the English a lot'. Only 9 per cent of 'equally Scottish and British' agree with the statement.

Table 10.3. Percentages of national identifiers and belief in government responsibility

	Scottish identifiers	British identifiers
Government should definitely spend more to create jobs	32	20
Government should definitely spend more to get rid of poverty	66	55
Government should definitely put more into National Health Service	75	64
Government should definitely spend more on education	69	58
Government should definitely or probably get rid of private education	32	20
Agree that income and wealth should be redistributed	66	50

the Conservative Party negatively. Table 10.4 reveals the relationship between national identity and party identity.

The extremes of national identity are quite highly correlated with Conservative and SNP identification. The more British people feel, the more likely they are to have a Conservative Party identity. Conversely, the stronger the Scottish identity, the stronger is the identification with the SNP. However, the SNP has not by any means captured the support of all those who see themselves as either more Scottish than British or even all of those who see themselves as exclusively Scottish. On the whole, there are similarities between Labour and SNP identifiers. Labour has considerable support among those who consider themselves exclusively Scottish, although the SNP do attract most of the support of this group. Overall, 50 per cent of the 'Brits' identify with the Conservatives while the Scottish identifiers are less loyal to one party – 43 per cent identify with Labour and 31 per cent with the SNP.

When it comes to the future constitutional status of Scotland, we would expect that those people who view themselves as more Scottish than British would be more inclined to support a Scottish parliament than 'more British than Scottish' respondents. Devolution, representing a measure of home rule short of independence, might be expected to have the support of those who see themselves as equally Scottish and British or at least identify in some measure with both Scottish and British dimensions.

As predicted, Scottish identifiers are more in favour of Scottish devolution and independence than are British identifiers (Table 10.5). But what is

Table 10.4. Percentages of national identifiers and party identities

	Scottish	More Scottish	Equal	More British	British
Conservative	15	20	48	53	67
Labour	35	47	35	32	25
Liberal Democrat	7	8	6	16	8
SNP	43	25	11	0	0

abundantly clear is the overwhelming level of support for a Scottish assembly among all groups. When we look at the two categories of British and Scottish identifiers we find that they reach a high level of agreement on the desired future constitutional status of Scotland: 53 per cent of Scottish identifiers and 49 per cent of British identifiers favour the creation of a Scottish parliament within Britain.

Conclusion: the political implications of national identity

In this chapter we have discussed how national identity relates to other identities and attitudes. In this concluding section we have taken the variables discussed above and, using regression analysis, sought to explain the significance of these in understanding the Scottish national identity (Table 10.6). Based on this analysis and the findings presented earlier in this chapter, we find that the Scottish national identity is most likely to be strong in the minds of non-religious, working-class males under the age of 55 who believe that government has a responsibility to be active in the economy. It is quite clear that the Scottish identity is intertwined with perceptions of England. The Scottish identifier has a tendency to 'dislike the English', no doubt partly explained by the strong conviction that the union brings more benefits to the English economy. These perceptions are manifested

Table 10.5. Percentages of national identifiers and favoured constitutional change

	Scottish	More Scottish	Equal	More British	British
Independent of Britain and Europe	14	6	2	3	4
Independent in Europe	31	19	10	6	0
Assembly	42	58	50	39	54
No change	13	17	38	52	42

Table 10.6. Regression analysis of national identity in Scotland

Independent variables	Regression coefficient with national identity
Age	-0.12*
Working class	0.05
Anti-English	0.11*
Pro-redistribution	0.06
Relative deprivation (England benefits more from union)	0.22*
Against Conservative Party	0.17*

$R^2 = 0.18$.
$N = 926$.
* Significant at the 0.01 level.

in attitudes towards parties and constitutional change. People with a strong Scottish identity are profoundly anti-Conservative. This would appear to rest on the belief that a Conservative government of Britain benefits England more than Scotland. Although Scottish identity is negatively related to Conservative identity, the SNP is not the sole beneficiary. Labour attracts a high level of support from the Scottish identifiers. Nor do Scottish identifiers demand separation from Britain. A Scottish parliament within Britain is the most favoured constitutional option. The factors underlying the Scottish national identity lead us to conclude that it is more than a cultural identity, that it has an important political dimension.

11

Party images in Scotland

Of the many explanations of voting behaviour which have been discussed in the literature in Britain, one which offers possibilities is that concerned with party image. The essence of this approach is that the elector's *general* perception of a party, its policies or political leader, rather than the detail of policy, is important in deciding how to vote. It seems unlikely that ordinary voters will be sufficiently well informed about policies to vote in response to them. Even if party policy is important to the individual voter, parties normally approach an election with a number of policies, making it difficult to single out one which really swings an election. The issue of trade union power may have been important in 1979, and Labour's policy on nuclear armaments may have had a malign effect on the fortunes of the Party in 1983, but on other occasions it is hard to single out a particular issue.

A number of studies have examined the importance of party image in British politics. One study focused on the Labour Party following the series of policy changes between 1987 and 1992, designed to make it more electorally attractive (Heath and Jowell 1994). While most electors could be expected to know little about the details of these changes, Heath and Jowell examined whether the 'synoptic' image of the Party had changed, in particular, whether the Party had changed from being seen as extreme to being moderate. They concluded that electors had indeed perceived a change in the Labour Party: it was regarded as more electable and consequently this helped it gain votes.

Crewe's study of partisan dealignment is also significant. Using the concept of 'statecraft' launched by Jim Bulpitt he suggested that 'cohesion, purpose, and success take precedence over policy and ideology in the voters' eyes' (Crewe 1988: 49). He presented evidence to suggest that electors did not become more Thatcherite during the period of that Prime Minister's government. On the contrary, the Labour Party was both unsuccessful at the polls and perceived as more in tune with the policy preferences of the voters. Against this, Margaret Thatcher's 'warrior style' seemed to find wider approval (Crewe 1988: 45).

Crewe and King (1994) looked at the images of Conservative and Labour leaders in the 1987 and 1992 elections, examining the proposition that leaders with a good image will increase the proportion of voters who support their parties, a kind of 'leadership bonus'. Largely using data from the 1987 and 1992 British elections, and incorporating the change in the Conservative leadership when Mr Major came in, they showed that there is strong evidence to support the importance of the leader's image for the standing of parties in the opinion of the electorate.

An analysis of party images in Scotland (Miller 1981) examined Scottish electors' views of party policies in Scotland, and how these differed from English attitudes. Miller compared the general perceptions of party policy positions (what voters think the parties stand for), evaluations of party policies (party with best policy), and the public image of relationships between parties (distance between parties). He found a remarkable similarity between Scottish and English respondents in perceptions of parties and issues (on British issues), but he identified quite significant differences in evaluations of these policies. He concluded that Scots 'evaluated the parties in a distinctive way' (1981: 118). Miller also noted that, compared with the English, Scots were rather less likely to see differences between the parties (1981: 126).

In this chapter, we examine some of the perceptions which electors had of the parties at the time of the 1992 general election. We examine general perceptions of party style, leadership and policy, comparing the nature of these perceptions in Scotland with those in England to see whether there are differences which explain the popularity of Labour north of the border compared with their bad showing in England.

Party style

Party image covers several different types of perception. There is, first of all, a more or less standard list of characteristics linked to models of the ways in which parties attract support: the style variables. Respondents are asked whether parties are:

- extreme or moderate
- united or divided
- good for one class or good for all classes
- capable of strong government or not capable of strong government
- caring or not caring

Roughly the same characteristics are asked about their leaders. In addition there are questions which sometimes apply to only one party, such as the extent to which a party is considered right or left of centre.

Table 11.1. Perceptions of parties 1992, Scotland (England) (%)

	Conservatives	Labour	Lib. Dem.	SNP
Extreme	38 (29)	30 (30)	8 (6)	51
Moderate	53 (62)	61 (60)	71 (75)	35
United	58 (68)	27 (30)	60 (70)	64
Divided	34 (24)	66 (61)	18 (13)	19
Good for one class	68 (53)	43 (56)	12 (10)	30
Good for all classes	28 (40)	47 (33)	63 (65)	48
Capable of strong government	79 (84)	44 (37)	25 (24)	30
Not capable of strong government	17 (12)	49 (56)	57 (56)	55
Caring	38 (48)	72 (70)	67 (74)	66
Uncaring	51 (40)	18 (17)	11 (7)	16

Table 11.1 displays responses to the questions on party style. Scottish and English respondents appear quite similar in the way they perceive the parties, the exception being the case of the Conservatives. Labour, overall, is seen as moderate, not extreme, caring but rather divided. However, Scottish respondents are more likely to regard Labour as being good for all classes and capable of strong government, hardly surprising given the higher level of support for Labour in Scotland. Perceptions of the Liberal Democrats, again, were similar: all respondents view them as moderate, united, good for all classes and caring, but not capable of strong government. If anything, Scots view the Liberal Democrats a little more negatively than English respondents, explained, perhaps, by the fact that 44 per cent are more likely to see the Liberal Democrats as 'closer to the Conservatives than Labour' compared with 39 per cent of English respondents.

When it comes to the Conservatives, perceptions of Scottish and English respondents are rather more divided. The Scots are more likely to see the Conservatives as extreme, divided, uncaring and good for one class only. They agree that the Party is capable of strong government. On the whole, the Conservatives in Scotland are definitely perceived less favourably in Scotland than in England. With this in mind, it is perhaps surprising to find that 29 per cent of Scots, compared with 33 per cent of English respondents, feel that differences between Labour and the Conservatives had decreased since the 1987 election.

The image of the SNP in Scotland is of a rather extreme party, not capable of strong government, but united in its cause, caring and as good for all classes as Labour. The Party is also seen as distinctly 'left wing': 42 per cent of the Scottish respondents described the SNP as left wing, 15 per cent right wing (with 18 per cent saying neither and 25 per cent not knowing).

The style variables explored above were put together in a simple Likert scale, where a 'positive' mention for each party – that it was moderate, united, good for all classes, capable of strong government, and caring – was awarded a point. Thus a respondent could award any of the parties analysed here from 0 to 5 points. Scottish Conservatives awarded their own party an average image score of 4.3. This is strikingly high compared with Labour electors' Labour image score of 3.0. The equivalent scores for the Liberal Democrats and the Nationalists were 3.6 and 2.6 respectively. It may be that the Conservative vote has been so reduced in Scotland that it is now confined to 'true believers', thus explaining their score. On the other hand, in a country where Labour has done so well the comparison is striking. The same could be said for the Nationalists. One might conclude that electors vote for Labour and the Nationalists but remain critical of them.

Party leaders

When we compare the party scores with those of the party leaders (Table 11.2) some interesting findings come to light. Kinnock, although seen as more 'extreme' than his party, is given similar scores in all other respects. Ashdown's scores reflect those of his party, although his personal strength as leader contrasts with his party's inability to persuade the voters that they are capable of strong government. Major scores much more highly than his party, particularly in Scotland; he is seen as much less 'extreme', more 'classless', and much more caring.

Based on these figures we suggest that Major was an asset for his party in 1992, in both Scotland and England. As previous research on Scottish attitudes has shown (Mitchell and Bennie 1996), perceptions of Major as Conservative leader showed a vast improvement on those of Thatcher. In 1989, nearly four Scots in every five (77 per cent) felt that Scots were

Table 11.2. Perceptions of party leaders 1992, Scotland (England) (%)

	Major	*Kinnock*	*Ashdown*
Extreme	20 (14)	40 (40)	17 (13)
Moderate	73 (80)	53 (51)	70 (75)
Looks after one class	54 (39)	41 (50)	13 (10)
Looks after all classes	41 (55)	52 (41)	67 (70)
Strong leader	63 (72)	42 (45)	61 (60)
Not a strong leader	32 (23)	53 (50)	25 (27)
Caring	69 (75)	77 (74)	77 (81)
Uncaring	25 (19)	17 (18)	10 (6)

treated as second-class citizens by Thatcher. Only 41 per cent indicated such a perception under Major in 1992 (Mitchell and Bennie 1996: 96). Furthermore, a comparison of attitudes towards Conservative leaders in 1987 and 1992 revealed that Thatcher was regarded as a strong but 'extreme' and 'uncaring' leader, who tended to look after one class only. Major, by comparison, was seen as much more moderate and caring, and more likely to look after all classes. For example, 75 per cent of Scots regarded Thatcher as 'extreme' in 1987 but only 20 per cent described Major in this way in 1992 (Mitchell and Bennie 1996: 97).

Despite the relative popularity of Major, the electoral position of the Conservatives in Scotland improved only marginally in 1992. This makes it difficult to arrive at a firm conclusion about the influence of the party leader's image. It is possible that images of party leaders are not very important determinants of electoral behaviour. Alternatively, the legacy of Margaret Thatcher in Scotland might have been so far reaching that the change in leadership made little impact. It is probable that the images of party leaders are so closely connected in the minds of voters with more general perceptions of party policy that it is practically impossible to separate the two. For this reason we now turn to party policies as perceived by the electorates in Scotland and England.

Party policy

In the 1992 Election Studies, Scottish and English respondents were asked a series of questions about particular policy issues. This allows us to assess general perceptions of party policies. In other words, what do voters think the parties stand for? Do the different electoral experiences of the parties in Scotland and England derive from different perceptions of party positions? Second, we compare the self-declared policy positions of voters in the two countries with the perceived positions of the parties. Are different voting patterns in Scotland the result of distinct issue priorities? Third, we consider the public image of the relationships between the parties in Scotland and England. Finally, we look at the perception of the parties in Scotland and the policy of constitutional reform.

Scottish and English respondents were presented with the following options in 1992:

• Some people feel that getting people back to work should be the government's top priority. Other people feel that keeping prices down should be the government's top priority.
• Some people feel that government should put up taxes a lot and spend much more on health and social services. Other people feel that

government should cut taxes a lot and spend much less on health and social services.
- Some people feel that government should nationalise many more private companies. Other people feel that government should sell off many more nationalised industries.
- Some people feel that government should make much greater efforts to make people's incomes more equal. Other people feel that government should be much less concerned about how equal people's incomes are.
- Some people feel that Britain should do all it can to unite fully with the European Community. Other people feel that Britain should do all it can to protect its independence from the European Community.
- Some people believe that we should spend much less money on defence. Others feel that defence spending should be greatly increased.
- Some people feel the government should see to it that every person has a job and a good standard of living. Others think the government should just let each person get ahead on their own.

The two options were placed at the opposite ends of a scale, and respondents were invited to choose a position for themselves and for the parties according to where they thought they or the parties stood on the issue.

Perceptions of party policies are compared in Table 11.3. We find that the responses of the Scottish and English respondents are, in fact, very similar. All the respondents share the view that the Labour Party is the party most likely to intervene in the economy, to create employment rather than keep prices down, to raise taxes for more spending on health, to nationalise rather than privatise, to spend less on defence and so on. The Conservatives are regarded as the least interventionist, with the Liberal Democrats somewhere between the two major parties on every issue. Only on the issue of Europe are the parties seen as being very close together. There is no evidence here to suggest that the Scots had a different view of what the parties stood for in 1992. This may have changed since then

Table 11.3. Perceived party policy positions, Scotland (England) (%)

Policy priority	Conservative	Labour	Lib. Dem.	SNP
Create work	34 (35)	79 (79)	54 (59)	65
Put up taxes and spend	24 (26)	81 (83)	61 (65)	62
Nationalise	17 (19)	66 (71)	31 (34)	48
Equalise income	21 (21)	77 (81)	52 (53)	63
For EC	43 (47)	47 (46)	44 (44)	42
Spend less on defence	32 (30)	62 (68)	45 (46)	55
Government role	37 (41)	75 (78)	53 (58)	64

Table 11.4. Respondents' policy positions in Scotland and England (%)

Policy priority	Scotland	England
Create work	76	70
Put up taxes and spend	68	64
Nationalise	47	37
Equalise incomes	69	56
For EC	51	43
Spend less on defence	53	43
Government's role	75	64

as Europe has become a more politically salient issue. The SNP, meanwhile, appear to be seen as a little more in favour of government intervention than the Liberal Democrats but not to the same extent as the Labour Party.

Although the Scots and English share a very similar understanding of party policies it is quite possible that they evaluate these policies in a different way. Table 11.4 displays the self-proclaimed policy positions of respondents in both countries. The Scots are more in favour of government action on the economy and welfare, a finding consistent with those documented in chapter 9 (rational voting) and chapter 10 (national identity). The self-placement of Scots on these issues is closest to the perceived policy image of Labour or the SNP.

From these results there seems to be fairly wide agreement between the views of Scottish voters and their perceptions of the parties' policies. To examine this relationship more closely, we were able to compare the respondents' position with their perception of the position of the party they voted for at the general election. For each issue we calculated the average difference between the preferences of respondents and the parties voted for. Table 11.5 shows the average differences between the views of respondents and the perception of their party policy for a number of the issues. The equivalent values for England are shown in (parentheses) in each cell.

It is striking that Conservative voters report the greatest distance between their own views and those of their chosen party. The differences between the Conservative 'distances' and those for the other parties is clear. For all the other parties, voters seem to feel closest to their perception of their own party's policies upon issues. However, this does not mean that they support these parties because of the policies reviewed. The evidence says nothing about the causal relationship between a respondent's issue position and their support for a particular party. In other words, we have to recognise that parties may in some way mould the views of their voters. For instance, the fact that SNP voters seem to feel closest to their perception of their own party's policies upon issues other than independence might be a

Table 11.5. Issue agreement and the vote in Scotland (England)

	Unemployment or prices	Taxes or services	Nationalise or privatise	Equality of income	Europe or Britain first
Conservatives	1.2 (1.4)	0.9 (1.3)	1.4 (1.1)	1.2 (0.9)	0.6 (0.8)
Labour	0.3 (0.1)	0.0 (0.3)	0.1 (0.8)	0.3 (0.5)	0.3 (0.6)
Liberal Democrats	0.3 (0.6)	0.2 (0.0)	0.1 (0.2)	0.0 (0.2)	0.8 (0.8)
SNP	0.0	0.1	0.1	0.2	0.3

reflection of genuine support for all these policies. But it is impossible to determine whether support for independence and the SNP in some way encourages voters to take on support for other SNP policy positions as they perceive them.

What are the implications of these findings for the parties in Scotland? The worry for the Conservatives is that perceptions of their policies in Scotland are far removed from the self-placement of Scots. Perceptions of Labour in 1992 were of a fairly radical party, likely to take responsibility for providing employment and a good standard of living for every person, rather than trusting in the free market. Whether such perceptions still hold true may have implications for Labour's support in Scotland.

Blair's approach has been to move Labour to the right. This has been as much about changing the Party's image as about changing its policies. In 1992, most respondents recognised a difference between Labour and the Conservatives: 53 per cent of Scottish and 55 per cent of English respondents thought there was a great deal of difference and 17 per cent of Scots thought there was not a great deal of difference, compared with 11 per cent of English respondents. We might expect to see a higher proportion of voters seeing no difference between the two parties in Britain as a whole but it will be interesting to see whether this occurs evenly across Britain.

In 1981 Miller argued that the Scottish Liberals 'had a public policy profile so fuzzy as to be almost invisible' (Miller 1981: 122). There is some evidence to suggest that voters are now more aware of Liberal Democrat policies. This fuzziness was most evident in the case of defence and Europe, which will be disappointing for the party as they have campaigned vigorously and distinctively on the issue of Europe. Miller found that around half of respondents had no idea what the Liberal and SNP policies were on nationalisation and spending on social services (Miller 1981: 118–19). In 1992 this figure had been reduced to only 10 per cent. Both the Liberal Democrats and the SNP still suffer from the fact that voters are unsure of their policies, though this was less the case in 1992 than it was previously.

Table 11.6. Perceptions of parties and constitutional reform in Scotland (%)

	Conservatives	*Labour*	*Lib. Dem.*	*SNP*	*All*
Independent from Britain/EC	1	4	3	37	6
Independence in EC	3	9	9	49	17
Assembly	18	62	45	5	50
No change	71	15	16	1	24
Other	1	1	1	0	1
Don't know	5	8	25	7	2
No answer	1	1	1	1	0

In the 1970s, four times as many respondents in both Scotland and England thought the Liberals were closer to the Conservatives than to Labour (Miller 1981: 27). The situation was more even in 1992: 44 per cent of Scots and 39 per cent of English respondents still thought that the Liberal Democrats were closer to the Conservatives, but 30 per cent of Scots and 33 per cent of English respondents thought they were now closer to Labour.

The SNP is now seen as the challenger to Labour on most issues, but not as 'left wing' on any issue. In the 1970s, 46 per cent of respondents were unable to place the SNP nearer to either the Conservatives or Labour; 37 per cent saw them as closer to Labour and 17 per cent saw them closer to the Conservatives (Miller 1981: 127). This had changed by 1992, with 63 per cent seeing the SNP as closer to Labour and only 14 per cent seeing the Party as closer to the Conservatives.

An examination of perceptions of the parties and constitutional change (Table 11.6) reveals that the SNP are clearly and accurately seen as the party of independence. Labour by 1992 had established itself as the party of devolution, followed by the Liberal Democrats. Miller noted that a third of respondents in 1974 did not know what the Liberal constitutional proposals were, despite their long-term commitment to a federal structure (Miller 1981: 122). In 1992 that figure had been reduced to a quarter. However, of all the parties, the Liberal Democrats are regarded with the greatest degree of uncertainty in this policy area.

Conclusion

It is tempting to conclude from this that the Scots may have different policy priorities and that they simply vote for the parties whose images are in line with these. However, the evidence presented in this chapter is far from clear cut. We suggest that it is more useful to explore party image in a more general sense, including perceptions of style, leadership and policy, particularly policies on constitutional reform. Once again we have to consider the territorial aspects of voting in Scotland. In 1992, there may have been a perception of the Conservatives as protectors of English interests and of Labour as a fairly radical, left-of-centre defender of Scottish interests. The key to change is likely to be the Labour Party. The change in its image which its leadership has tried to foster may have altered not only perceptions of the Party but also the nature of its support. This does not mean that a more right-wing image would necessarily damage it electorally in 1997 but it may compound problems if after taking office it is perceived to have failed to govern effectively or in Scotland's interests.

12

The political future and home rule in Scotland

Scottish home rule has been a common theme of this book. It lies behind most topics in the political debate. It is not the highest priority issue for electors, but most Scottish adults support constitutional change in one form or another. More recently there has been a significant change among the political élites in Scotland, and home rule has, in a way, become a key to understanding Scottish politics.

For that reason we conclude the book with an analysis of our findings in this field. We shall trace its links with other topics, such as the importance of class, the significance of religion for political attitudes, and the central place of national identity. We do not argue that the demand for home rule has a revolutionary effect on the way Scots think about politics, but we believe that these other topics, such as class, the attitude to individual issues and the fortunes of the major parties, can only be understood if we remember that Scottish politicians must be seen to take a clear position on the topic, and one that is consistent with the interests of the majority of their potential supporters.

Home rule in Scottish politics

Home rule has been at the heart of Scottish politics for a quarter of a century. Before that, the debate grumbled on for more than a century. It is the most serious attempt to establish responsible regional government within Britain, and has a political basis which is different from that in other British regions. This has implications for the resolution of the problem, and perhaps for the establishment of regional institutions elsewhere. In summary, interest in constitutional change is fuelled by a form of nationalism, unlike the interest in regionalism in England.

It is necessary to say something about the terminology used. In the mid to late 1970s, 'devolution' was the term describing plans for establishing a Scottish parliament or assembly which would control some governmental powers only or principally affecting Scotland. Other powers would remain within the competence of Westminster, which would retain overall control. There was controversy over what these powers were, and about such things as the status of the assembly: whether it should be part of a federal scheme, for example. Devolution was strictly distinguished from independence, where a government of Scotland would be responsible for every government service which affected the country, since Scotland would have separated from Britain. In this chapter we shall use the term 'home rule' to cover the relationships short of complete independence, because, first of all, 'home rule' is now the most widely used term, and secondly to draw attention to a certain fuzziness between support for limited powers for Scotland and support for complete independence; 'home rule' describes a Scottish parliament with all the powers proposed for the assembly in 1979, and many more. Federalism is short of independence, but far beyond the devolution of the 1970s, and is one of the possible arrangements which come under the heading of 'home rule'. The possibility of Scotland being a partner with England and the other EU countries became more important in the 1980s, and complicated the situation yet further. Many recognised that voters might support Scottish autonomy short of independence as a prelude to independence. 'Home rule' therefore covers all degrees of power holding short of independence, either inside or outwith the EU.

A general model of support for Scottish home rule lies behind our analysis. Support for this programme is inevitably élite led. It does, however, depend on a strong sentiment of Scottishness, which is not necessarily political. Since the 1960s this sentiment has been partially politicised from time to time, by the activities of certain Scottish élites. Popular support for home rule thus depends on identity, rather than on a rational choice for an arrangement that might improve economic or other conditions. In addition, Scottish identity may compete with class or party identity, which is the basis of Labour's strength in Scotland (as argued in chapter 7). If Labour is not able to 'capture' it, national identity may pose a threat to Labour's future. This certainly accounts for the efforts of Labour to build its image as a Scottish party (Table 12.1) and, as we have seen (chapters 4, 5, 6 and 11), the other Scottish parties have followed the same path.

There is another important part to our model. Identity is contextually determined. In one context we may feel that we are Catholics rather than Scots; in another we may be British in opposition to the exigencies of the Commission in Brussels. Scottish identity may take on a political meaning only when there are features in our context which make the political meaning important. Such a feature was the imposition of an unpopular poll tax by what was perceived to be an English government. Another feature would be the existence of an institution, a party perhaps,

Table 12.1. Labour voters' perception of Labour's view on home rule in 1979 and 1992 (%)

	1979	*1992*
Independence (for 1992, in or out of Europe)	4	15
Assembly	72	73
No change	23	14

which drew attention to the political dimension of the identity. There might also be chance events, such as the death of a leader. Thus the nature of what an actor considers to be his or her identity, or his or her rational interest even, is not stable. It remains dependent on perceptions of that condition and these, in turn, are structured in various ways, by various agencies.

Support for home rule

About three-quarters of Scottish voters have supported home rule or independence ever since the first recorded polling on the subject in 1947 (Mitchell 1996). This proportion has not materially changed, even during the days of the SNP's greatest successes. Opinion polls suggested that under one-fifth supported independence until the mid-1980s, when the percentage of supporters rose. Especially in the case of home rule, there is a problem because the questions used differed in different surveys. Even with the same wording, they would have been taken to refer to contemporary proposals, which have changed. Even independence means something different now with the arrival of the EU. In the 1979 Scottish Election Study, respondents were asked which of a range of options they would prefer (see Table 12.2). The survey in 1979 recorded a drop from the normal figure of around 20 per cent supporting independence, suggesting that minds had been concentrated by the referendum.

Table 12.2. Constitutional preferences, 1979

	%
No devolution	13
Ad hoc parliamentary committees in Scotland	16
A Scottish assembly with control over some Scottish affairs	32
A Scottish assembly with control over most Scottish affairs	30
A completely independent Scotland	8

Table 12.3. Constitutional preferences, 1992

	%
No change	24
An assembly	52
Scotland independent of Britain but within Europe	18
Scotland independent of Britain and Europe	6

In 1992 the questionnaire provided four choices (Table 12.3). This formulation was a better reflection of the options actually on offer, but it is impossible to make any but the vaguest comparisons. The proportions in favour of either 'no change' or 'independence' seem to have gone up. Looking at either set of results, however, there is a massive majority for constitutional change in the direction of home rule of some sort. It should also be pointed out that these opinions are expressed in terms of relatively specific proposals for change. This is quite different from the questions in several enquiries in England which have elicited quite extensive support for more power for 'their part of Britain' or some other phrase, where we are unclear what the respondent takes as a referent, either to the region or to the sorts of powers which are meant. In terms of research methodology, the questions in Scotland and England are not comparable.

Even a large majority favouring a course of action must be looked at carefully. Governments have to implement many policies of differing importance to politicians and to the public. When respondents were asked in 1979 about the importance of the devolution legislation to their vote, 22 per cent said that it was extremely important, 37 per cent said that it was fairly important, and 41 per cent said that it was not important at all. When asked to name key issues by opinion pollsters, Scottish electors generally place home rule fairly low on the list.

However, we have to be careful with these data. It has been shown that in the 1983, 1987 and 1992 elections, had British voters supported the party they considered best able to handle the issue they believed most important, then Labour would have done much better. In 1983, Labour and Conservatives would have received equal shares of the vote instead of a 15 per cent lead for the Tories. The 'issue voting' hypothesis is not sustained by the evidence (Sanders 1992: 194). In addition, it is quite conceivable that unemployment is perceived to be the most important issue for some Scottish voters and as a consequence of this they support constitutional change. The list of salient issues is one of the least reliable ways of predicting voting behaviour. A more reliable guide to political salience is the degree of consistency voters attach to an issue. In this respect, home rule and constitutional politics would appear to have become firmly part of the political furniture of contemporary Scottish politics.

Scottish identity in the political struggle

In this section, we shall examine how Scottish identity has become part of British politics, and how it has taken on a life of its own. In recent times when home rule has been debated, it was seldom out of the front pages of the *Glasgow Herald* or the *Scotsman* and it was also a major topic on the Scottish television networks. The sympathies of the newspapers were quite clearly in favour of home rule, and it was not difficult to work out similar attitudes among major television commentators. For these reasons and others, including high-profile modern cultural developments in various forms until the present day, Scottish identity is well defined. The country's political, economic and cultural history has ensured the existence of a 'community of fate' (Anderson 1991). We have seen, however, that this did not push national self-government anywhere near the top of the agenda for the majority of Scottish voters.

The rise of the SNP forced Labour to adopt a devolution policy in the 1970s despite the existence of a substantial number of Labour opponents of home rule. To appease these anti-devolutionists, the Labour government agreed to hold a referendum on its proposals in 1979. Only 47 per cent of Labour voters voted 'yes' despite the official stance of the Party. Under the terms of the legislation, 40 per cent of the eligible electorate had to vote 'yes', otherwise the government was obliged to move an order to repeal the devolution legislation. A narrow majority of those who turned out to vote voted in favour of devolution. However, the proportion of the total electorate was only 33 per cent (on the turnout on the day, there would have to have been a 65 per cent 'yes' vote to meet the 40 per cent requirement).

Supporters of devolution were devastated by the result. The 1979 general election further damaged morale among home rulers when Labour was thrown out of office and the eleven Nationalist MPs were reduced to two. Devolution appeared to be dead. The cross-party CSA was set up by a small group of supporters in September 1979 and tried hard to raise popular interest through rallies, fetes, and conferences all over Scotland, but attendances were very small. Labour was extremely cautious about being too closely associated with the CSA, although it was approached many times. A few constituency organisations joined, but the Scottish executive maintained that the Party never joined an organisation which it did not lead. This was precisely what other parties wanted to avoid. Again, although many individual Nationalists were members of the CSA, the official SNP line was that the CSA stood for devolution, and was of no relevance to the fight for independence. There were even individual Conservative members, but not many. By contrast, the Liberals and the Communist Party were committed and active forces behind the CSA. A strong Communist presence in the Scottish trade unions was part of the reason why the STUC and individual unions, like the NUM, were active in the CSA when other élites were so uninterested. The churches were also sympathetic. Though there were strong unionists among the clergy, the Church and Nation Committee of the Church of Scotland had long ago made a deliberation in favour of a Scottish parliament. It is significant that the chairperson of the Scottish Constitutional Convention, which we shall discuss below, was Canon Kenyon Wright.

Even with all the goodwill and sympathy, few people expected that there would be much movement towards home rule in the early 1980s. Interest and support for home rule began to grow within the Labour Party from about 1983. In the later 1980s, the impetus for this change was largely the realisation that, however large the Labour majority was in Scotland, under the existing arrangements they had no effect on Scottish policy. As we have seen elsewhere in this book, Labour took more and more seats in Scotland until, at the 1987 election, they won fifty of the seventy-two, but, in terms of influence on policy, they were still powerless. This realisation itself was a potent argument in favour of home rule. Converts to the cause included high-profile former opponents like Robin Cook. Labour MPs, such as Dennis Canavan, who had long supported devolution became more active. Following the election, the Party introduced a Scotland bill, which was, of course, defeated, but which was meant to re-emphasise Labour's commitment to the principle of home rule. It was a campaigning device rather than a serious piece of thinking about change in the constitution, but it did mark a move towards more active support.

In July 1988, the CSA launched a radical document entitled *A Claim of Right for Scotland*. It had been put together by Jim Ross, a retired senior civil servant in the Scottish Office, who had been secretary of a committee which drew up plans for the devolution legislation in the last Labour government. The basis of its argument was that the existing British government had no legitimacy in Scotland because sovereignty was in the hands of the Scottish people. On this basis it demanded a Scottish constitutional convention which would embody this Scottish sovereignty, and decide upon the future of Scotland.

Such a frontal assault on British constitutional theory was not immediately welcomed by Labour, but on 21 October the shadow Scottish Secretary, Donald Dewar, addressed a meeting in the University of Stirling, announcing that Labour would participate. The Scottish executive had called for a positive response to a consultation on the subject, and the grass-roots Party turned out to be more than enthusiastic. Neil Kinnock did not even mention plans for Scottish home rule when he spoke to the Scottish Labour Party conference, and when he was asked to comment on this omission in a television interview, he said that he had not mentioned lots of other things, 'including environmental conditions in the Himalayas'. The Labour Party in Scotland now supported a much more extensive plan for home rule than that set out in the 1979 bill, and did so because there was a clear majority at all levels of the Party for it.

In November 1988, the SNP overturned a huge Labour majority and won a by-election in Glasgow, Govan. The SNP decided not to participate in the Convention, fearing that it would be used by Labour to avoid taking action on devolution and used to undermine the SNP's case for independence in Europe. The importance of the Convention was that, for the first time, Labour and the Liberal Democrats sat down together with the representatives of the unions, the churches, local government, and many other interests in Scotland and worked out a common scheme for home rule. The Convention of Scottish Local Authorities acted as secretariat, bringing credibility and skill to the Convention. The Convention reconciled, to some extent, the devolutionary scheme of Labour with the federalism of the Liberal Democrats. The Convention and its final report (Constitutional Convention 1990) represented a substantial level of agreement on the part of important Scottish political and other institutions about the constitutional future of the country. Labour was even prepared to move towards the Liberal Democrats' demands for proportional representation in the planned Scottish parliament, though they did not agree to this for Westminster elections. More than this, the Labour Party, which had adopted devolution before 1979 as a device to save its votes, now contained few public dissidents on this issue, and a growing number of members were enthusiasts for the idea, even for independence. About 20 per cent of Labour voters actually supported independence in 1992, an advance from about 8 per cent in 1979. Even short of independence, political opinion had gone a long way beyond devolution. The final report of the Convention demanded that, once established, the powers of the Scottish parliament should be entrenched, so that they could not be changed without the consent of the parliamentary representatives of the people of Scotland (Kellas 1992; Mitchell 1991, 1996). All this seemed to promise home rule as a certainty at the 1992 election, because the opinion polls had, almost to the end, all predicted a safe Labour victory.

Home rule and the threat to the existing system

In the 1960s and 1970s the majority of Labour and Liberal politicians supported home rule to save their seats. Over the years, devolution and home rule have become part of Scottish political discourse. There was little association of the policy with parties other than the SNP. This has changed.

As the Scottish Election Study results reveal, there is a strong relationship between Labour and Liberal Democrat voting and support for an assembly. It should be noted that the proportion of Labour voters in this category is only (marginally) lower than that for the Liberal Democrats because a higher proportion of Labour voters support independence. In any case, Labour, as by far the larger party, has certainly been more prominent in the campaign and has dominated the media in its support for home rule. Thus even though pride in Scotland is not sparked off by political features (chapter 10), and though it is not among the most important policies for voters, it is clearly associated in Labour voters' minds with their own party. Since 1979, the proportion of Labour voters perceiving that Labour supported an assembly has not changed, but a lower percentage believed that Labour supported the status quo and a higher one thought that Labour supported independence (see Table 12.1).

It is consistent with this that voters support devolution at least partly because it is a Labour policy. In this context, the identity model of policy choice seems the most appropriate. This would explain the consistent support of Labour voters. What enthusiasm there was among Labour voters may be challenged even more by the sudden decision of the Labour leadership in June 1996 to change their commitment to introduce a bill for a Scottish parliament in their first term in office without a referendum. A referendum would be held, not only for the principle of a parliament, but also for the issue of its powers to raise up to three pence in the pound in tax. There has been great discontent among Labour activists about this change and because of the way in which it was announced, without consultation. At face value, it looked like a capitulation to the Conservatives, and many Tory leaders in Scotland were surprised by this unlooked for gift. It also looked like a repudiation of the years of work which Labour in Scotland had devoted to its partners in the Constitutional Convention. At a time when Conservative morale was rising in Scotland and the economic indicators seemed to be going their way, the Labour leadership faced the real difficulty that a discontented membership in Scotland might not work in a future election with conviction. In these circumstances both the Labour vote could go down and the Conservatives could begin to recover.

Conclusion

At the beginning of this chapter we suggested that identity was contextual. One of the most important aspects of any social context are the institutions which structure the situation for the individual. For party supporters the party will be very important. It does not, however, explain everything.

Before 1974, the Labour Party was opposed to devolution, and yet, as we pointed out at the beginning of this chapter, the level of support for devolution or home rule had already reached 75 per cent, as far back as 1947. We suggest that the important feature of the present situation is that the Labour Party has structured home rule as a possible line of development, and as part of a mainstream political programme. It did not have this status before 1974. Labour's continuing commitment to the policy in the Constitutional Convention reinforced this. This does not seem to have increased the level of popular enthusiasm, although one would expect rather fewer Labour voters to reject the assembly than did in 1979. It has, however, brought in élites from pressure groups and other public bodies.

All this attempts to explain the support for devolution at the level of élite support, but it is not enough. It ignores the fact that Labour first got into the game of home rule because the SNP started to attract votes, which threatened Labour votes. The performance of the SNP at elections has been very patchy, but a large proportion of Scottish electors have, since 1970, voted for them regularly. Over half of all Scottish electors, irrespective of who they voted for, or their views on the constitutional issue, said in 1974, 1979, and 1992 that they believed that the SNP had been good for Scotland. This suggests that awareness of Scottish identity does play a role now. Even though the political element of Scottish feeling is, as we saw, not very prominent, there is a sense that Scotland does have interests which are not always given due attention (chapter 10). If electors had wanted to register a protest, they could have voted for the Liberal Democrats, but they voted SNP, which suggests that a sizeable number felt that Scottishness was an alternative basis of political identity and action.

The existence of the SNP has forced Labour to pay attention to Scottish matters. In recent elections, the SNP has threatened the class base of Labour's support as much as its appeal as a Scottish party. By reacting to the threat of the SNP, the Labour Party has made the political aspect of Scottish identity even more prominent.

None of the foregoing necessarily points to an inevitable further increase of Scottish political identity. It suffered radical setbacks at the elections of 1979 and 1992, and there could be more in the future. What the last two decades do suggest is that Scottish political identity is not likely to go away, because structural features build it into the political discourse. Scottish voters have not taken this to mean that home rule should be high on their collective agenda, but the conditions which we have outlined make it very possible that other developments might precipitate the voters in this direction. Another incident like the imposition of the poll tax – water privatisation, for example, or a further defeat for the Labour Party in the next general election – could easily perform this function.

Bibliography

Anderson, B. (1991) *Imagined Communities*, London, Verso.

Balfour, Lord (1954) *Report of the Royal Commission on Scottish Affairs 1952–54*, Cmd 9212, London, HMSO.

Bealey, F. (1970) *The Social and Political Thought of the British Labour Party*, London, Weidenfeld and Nicholson.

Beer, S. (1965) *Modern British Politics*, London, Faber & Faber.

Beer, S. (1982) *Britain Against Itself*, London, Faber & Faber.

Bell, D. and S. Dow (1995) 'Economic policy options for a Scottish parliament', *Scottish Affairs*, no. 13, 42–67.

Bell, I. (1993) 'Publishing, journalism and broadcasting', in Paul Scott (ed.), *Scotland: A Concise Cultural History*, Edinburgh, Mainstream, 385–95.

Bochel, J. and D. Denver (1970) 'Religion and voting: a critical review and a new analysis', *Political Studies*, vol. 18, 205–19.

Bochel, J. and D. Denver (1978) 'The regional council elections of May 1978', in N. Drucker and H. M. Drucker (eds), *The Scottish Government Yearbook, 1979*, Edinburgh, Paul Harris, 140–56.

Bradley, I. (1981) *Breaking the Mould? The Birth and Prospects of the Social Democratic Party*, Oxford, Martin Robertson.

Brand, J. (1978) *The National Movement in Scotland*, London, Routledge.

Brand, J., D. McLean and W. Miller (1983) 'The birth and death of a three-party system: Scotland in the seventies', *British Journal of Political Science*, vol. 13, 463–88.

Brand, J., J. Mitchell and P. Surridge (1993) 'Identity and the vote: class and nationality in Scotland', in P. Norris *et al.* (eds), *British Elections and Parties Yearbook 1993*, Hemel Hempstead, Harvester Wheatsheaf, 143–57.

Brand, J., J. Mitchell and P. Surridge (1994) 'Will Scotland come to the aid of the party?', in Anthony Heath *et al.*, *Labour's Last Chance? The 1992 Election and Beyond*, Aldershot, Dartmouth, 213–28.

Brown, A., D. McCrone and L. Paterson (1996) *Politics and Society in Scotland*, Houndmills, Macmillan.

Brown, G. (1981) *The Labour Party and Political Change in Scotland, 1918–1929*, unpublished PhD, Edinburgh University.

Butler, D. (1988) 'The 1987 general election in historical perspective', in R. Skidelsky (ed.), *Thatcherism*, London, Chatto & Windus, 65–78.

Butler, D. (1993) *British General Elections since 1945*, Oxford, Basil Blackwell.

Butler, D. and D. Stokes (1974) *Political Change in Britain*, revised edn, London, Macmillan.

Butler, D. and D. Kavanagh (1992) *The British General Election of 1992*, Houndmills, Macmillan.

Butler, D., A. Adonis and T. Travers (1994) *Failure in British Government: The Politics of the Poll Tax*, Oxford, Oxford University Press.

Cairncross, A. (1992) *The British Economy since 1945*, Oxford, Blackwell.

Central Statistical Office (CSO) (1995) *Regional Trends No. 30*, London, HMSO.

Chrimes, S. B. (ed.) (1950) *The General Election in Glasgow, February 1950*, Glasgow, Jackson, Son and Company.

Constitutional Convention (1990) *Towards Scotland's Parliament*, Edinburgh, Constitutional Convention.

Cook, C. (1993) *A Short History of the Liberal Party*, 4th edn, London, Macmillan.

Coupland, Sir R. (1954) *Welsh and Scottish Nationalism*, London, Collins.

Crewe, I. (1988) 'Partisan alignment ten years on', in Hugh Berrington (ed.), *Change in British Politics*, London, Frank Cass.

Crewe, I. (1992) 'The 1987 general election', in D. Denver and G. Hands (eds), *Issues and Controversies in British Electoral Behaviour*, Hemel Hempstead, Harvester Wheatsheaf, 343–55.

Crewe, I. and D. Denver (1985) *Electoral Change in Western Democracies*, London, Croom Helm.

Crewe, I. and A. King (1994) 'Did Major win? Did Kinnock lose? Leadership effects in the 1992 election', in Anthony Heath *et al.*, *Labour's Last Chance? The 1992 Election and Beyond*, Aldershot, Dartmouth, 125–48.

Crowley, D. W. (1956) 'The Crofters' Party, 1885–1892', *Scottish Historical Review*, vol. 35, 110–26.

Curtice, J. (1996) 'Should Britain follow the Caledonian way?', in Iain McLean and David Butler (eds), *Fixing the Boundaries: Defining and Redefining Single-Member Electoral Districts*, Aldershot, Dartmouth, 235–50.

Curtice, J. and H. Semetko (1994) 'Does it matter what the papers say?', in Anthony Heath *et al.*, *Labour's Last Chance? The 1992 Election and Beyond*, Aldershot, Dartmouth, 43–64.

Cyr, A. (1988) *Liberal Politics in Britain*, New Brunswick, NY, Transaction Books.

Dalton, R. (1988) *Citizen Politics in Western Democracies*, Chatham, NJ, Chatham House Publishers.

Dalton, R. (1996) *Citizen Politics: Public Opinion and Political Parties in Advanced Industrial Democracies*, Chatham, NJ, Chatham House Publishers.

Dalton, R. and M. Kuechler (1990) *Challenging the Political Order: New Social and Political Movements in Western Democracies*, Cambridge, Polity.

Danson, M., G. Lloyd, and D. Newlands (1989) '"Scottish enterprise": the creation of a more effective development agency or the pursuit of ideology?', *Quarterly Economic Commentary*, vol. 14, 70–5.

Denver, D. (1994) *Elections and Voting Behaviour in Britain*, Hemel Hempstead, Harvester Wheatsheaf.

Denver, D. and G. Hands (1992) *Issues and Controversies in British Electoral Behaviour*, Hemel Hempstead, Harvester Wheatsheaf.

Denver, D. and H. Bochel (1994) 'The last act: the regional elections of 1994', *Scottish Affairs*, no. 9, 68–79.

Denver, D. and H. Bochel (1995) 'Catastrophe for the Conservatives: the council elections of 1995', *Scottish Affairs*, no. 13, 27–41.

Drucker, H. M. (1979) *Doctrine and Ethos in the Labour Party*, London, Allen and Unwin.

Dunleavy, P. and C. Husbands (1985) *British Democracy at the Crossroads: Voting and Party Competition in the 1980s*, London, Allen and Unwin.

Finlay, R. (1994) *Independent and Free, Scottish Politics and the Origins of the Scottish National Party, 1918–1945*, Edinburgh, John Donald.

Fisher, J. (1996) *British Political Parties*, Hemel Hempstead, Prentice Hall.

Garner, R. and R. Kelly (1993) *British Political Parties Today*, Manchester, Manchester University Press.

Garrett, G. (1994) 'Popular capitalism: the electoral legacy of Thatcherism', in Anthony Heath *et al.*, *Labour's Last Chance? The 1992 Election and Beyond*, Aldershot, Dartmouth, 107–24.

Gellner, E. (1983) *Nations and Nationalism*, Oxford, Blackwell.

Greeley, A. (1992) 'Religion in Britain, Ireland and the USA', *British Social Attitudes, 9th Report*, Aldershot, Dartmouth, 51–70.

Hanham, H. J. (1965) 'The creation of the Scottish Office, 1881–87', *Juridical Review*, 205–44.

Hanham, H. J. (1969) *Scottish Nationalism*, London, Faber & Faber.

Harrop, M. (1986) 'Press coverage of post-war British elections', in I. Crewe and M. Harrop (eds), *Political Communications: The General Election Campaign of 1983*, Cambridge, Cambridge University Press, 137–49.

Harvie, C. (1993) *No Gods and Precious Few Heroes*, Edinburgh, Edinburgh University Press.

Heath, A. F., R. M. Jowell and J. K. Curtice (1985) *How Britain Votes*, Oxford, Pergamon.

Heath, A. F., R. M. Jowell and J. K. Curtice (1991) *Understanding Political Change*, Oxford, Pergamon.

Heath, A. F. and R. Jowell (1994) 'Labour's policy review', in A. Heath *et al.*, *Labour's Last Chance? The 1992 Election and Beyond*, Aldershot, Dartmouth, 191–212.

Heath, A. F., R. Jowell and J. Curtice (eds) (1994) *Labour's Last Chance? The 1992 Election and Beyond*, Aldershot, Dartmouth.

Hetherington, A. (1992) *Inside the BBC, 1975–1980: A Personal View*, Glasgow, Whitewater Press.

HMSO (1937) *Report of the Committee on Scottish Administration*, Cmd 5563, Edinburgh, HMSO.

Holland, R. (1991) *The Pursuit of Greatness: Britain and the World Role, 1900–1970*, London, Fontana Press.

House of Commons (1990) *Working of Select Committee System*, Procedure Committee Report, London, House of Commons, 19.

Inglehart, R. (1977) *The Silent Revolution*, Princeton, NJ, Princeton University Press.

Inglehart, R. (1990) *Culture Shift in Advanced Industrial Society*, Princeton, NJ, Princeton University Press.

Johnston, R. (1979) *Scottish Liberal Party Speeches 1971–1978*, Inverness, Bookmag.

Kamenka, E. (1993) 'Nationalism: ambiguous legacies and contingent futures', *Political Studies*, vol. 41, 78–92.

Keating, M. (1975) *The Role of the Scottish MP in the Scottish Political System, in the UK Political System and in the Relationship Between the Two*, unpublished PhD thesis, CNAA.

Keating, M. and D. Bleiman (1979) *Labour and Scottish Nationalism*, London, Macmillan.

Kellas, J. (1989) *The Scottish Political System*, 4th edn, Cambridge, Cambridge University Press.

Kellas, J. (1992) 'The Scottish Constitutional Convention', *Scottish Government Yearbook, 1992*, Edinburgh, Edinburgh University Press, 50–8.

Kemp, A. (1993) *The Hollow Drum, Scotland Since the War*, Edinburgh, Mainstream.

Lang, I. and B. Henderson (1975) *The Scottish Conservatives: A Past and a Future*, Edinburgh, Scottish Conservative and Unionist Association.

Linklater, M. (1992) 'The media', in M. Linklater and R. Denniston (eds), *Chambers Anatomy of Scotland*, Edinburgh, Chambers, 126–44.

Lipset, S. M. and S. Rokkan (eds) (1967) *Party Systems and Voter Alignments: Cross-National Perspectives*, London, Collier-Macmillan.

Loosemore, J. and V. J. Hanby (1971) 'The theoretical limits of maximum distortion', *British Journal of Political Science*, vol. 1, 467–77.

MacCormick, J. (1955) *The Flag in the Wind*, London, Victor Gollancz.

McCrone, D. (1992) *Understanding Scotland*, London, Routledge.

McCrone, G. (1965) *Scotland's Economic Progress, 1951–60*, London, Allen & Unwin.

McDowell, W. H. (1992) *The History of BBC Broadcasting in Scotland, 1923–1983*, Edinburgh, Edinburgh University Press.

McLean, I. (1970) 'The rise and fall of the Scottish National Party', *Political Studies*, vol. 18, 367–72.

McLean, R. (not dated) *Labour and Scottish Home Rule*, Broxburn, Scottish Labour Action.

McPherson, A. and C. Raab (1988) *Governing Education: A Sociology of Policy Since 1945*, Edinburgh, Edinburgh University Press.

Mény, Y. (1991) *Government and Politics in Western Europe*, Oxford, Oxford University Press.

Miller, W. (1981) *The End of British Politics?* Oxford, Clarendon Press.

Miller, W. (1991) *Media and Voters*, Oxford, Clarendon Press.

Miller, W., J. Brand and M. Jordan (1981) 'Government without a mandate: its causes and consequences for the Conservative Party in Scotland', *Political Quarterly*, vol. 52, 203–13.

Mitchell, J. (1990) *Conservatives and the Union*, Edinburgh, Edinburgh University Press.

Mitchell, J. (1991) 'Constitutional conventions and the Scottish national movement: origins, agenda and outcomes', *Strathclyde Papers on Government and Politics*, no. 78.

Mitchell, J. (1996) *Strategies for Self-government*, Edinburgh, Polygon.

Mitchell, J. and L. Bennie (1996) 'Thatcherism and the Scottish question', in *British Elections and Parties Yearbook, 1995*, London, Frank Cass, 90–104.

Müller-Rommel, F. (1989) *New Politics in Western Europe: The Rise and Success of Green Parties and Alternative Lists*, Boulder, CO, Westview Press.

Munro, R. (1930) *Looking Back: Fugitive Writings and Sayings*, London, Thomas Nelson.

Norris, P. (1995) 'Labour Party quotas for women', *British Elections and Parties Yearbook, 1994*, London, Frank Cass, 167–80.

Norton, P. (1994) 'The parliamentary party and party committees', in Anthony Seldon and Stuart Bell (eds), *Conservative Century: the Conservative Party since 1900*, Oxford, Oxford University Press.

Pitchford, R. and T. Greaves (1989) *Merger: The Inside Story*, Winewall, Liberal Renewal.

Richardson, D. and C. Rootes (eds) (1995) *The Green Challenge: The Development of Green Parties in Europe*, London, Routledge.

Rokkan, S. and D. Urwin (1982) *The Politics of Territorial Identity: Studies in European Regionalism*, London, Sage.

Rokkan, S. and D. Urwin (1983) *Economy, Territory, Identity*, London, Sage.

Rose, R. and I. McAllister (1986) *Voters Begin to Choose: From Closed Class to Open Elections in Britain*, London, Sage.

Sanders, D. (1992) 'Why the Conservative Party won – again', in Anthony King *et al.* (eds), *Britain at the Polls 1992*, Chatham, NJ, Chatham House Publishers, 171–222.

Sanders, D. (1993) 'Forecasting the 1992 general election outcome: the performance of an economic model', in D. Denver, P. Norris, D. Broughton and C. Rallings (eds), *British Elections and Parties Yearbook 1993*, Hemel Hempstead, Harvester Wheatsheaf, 100–15.

Sartori, G. (1976) *Parties and Party Systems: A Framework for Analysis*, Cambridge, Cambridge University Press.

Schmitt, M. and S. Holmberg (1995) 'Political parties in decline?', in M. Klingemann and D. Fuchs (eds), *Beliefs in Government, Vol. 1: Citizens and the State*, Oxford, Oxford University Press, 95–133.

Scottish Local Government Information Unit (SLGIU) (1991) 'Case for change not proven', *Scottish Local Government*, no. 42, September.

Scottish Trades Union Congress (STUC) (1987) *Scotland: A Land Fit For Heroes*, Glasgow, STUC.

Seawright, D. (1996) 'The Scottish Unionist Party: what's in a name?', *Scottish Affairs*, no. 14, 90–102.

Seawright, D. and J. Curtice (1995) 'The decline of the Scottish Conservative and Unionist Party, 1950–92: religion, ideology or economics?', *Contemporary Record*, vol. 9, no. 2, 319–42.

Sillars, J. (1986) *The Case for Optimism*, Edinburgh, Polygon.

Simmel, G. (1966) *Conflict and the Web of Group Affiliation*, New York, Free Press.

Skelton, N. (1924) *Constructive Conservatism*, Edinburgh, Wm Blackwood.

Skinner, M. (1967) 'Catholic elementary education in Glasgow, 1818–1918', in T. R. Bone (ed.), *Studies in the History of Scottish Education, 1872–1939*, London, University of London Press, 13–70.

Smith, A. (1991) *National Identity*, London, Penguin.

Steed, M. (1979) 'The Liberal Party', in H. M. Drucker (ed.), *Multi-Party Britain*, London, Macmillan, 76–106.

165

Stovall, J. G. (1978) *The Scottish Press and Nationalism: A Content Analysis of Newspaper Attention to Nationalism, 1966–78*, unpublished PhD, University of Tennessee.

Thatcher, M. (1993) *The Downing Street Years*, London, HarperCollins.

Urwin, D. (1966) 'Scottish conservatism: a party organisation in transition', *Political Studies*, vol. 14, 145–62.

Urwin, D. (1994) 'Back to the future – again? A reassessment of minority nationalism in Western democracies', *Journal of Behavioral and Social Sciences*, 1994, no. 3, 1–23.

Warner, G. (1988) *The Scottish Tory Party: A History*, London, Weidenfeld and Nicolson.

Wheatley, Lord (1969) *Report of the Royal Commission on Local Government in Scotland*, London, HMSO.

Young, J. (1993) *Britain and European Unity, 1945–92*, Houndmills, Macmillan.

Index